The Little Flower of Nashville

The Little Flower of Nashville

The Story of Rosemary Thérèse Robinson

by Hayley Robinson Shovlin

Foreword by Jimmy Mitchell

The Little Flower of Nashville LLC
Nashville, Tennessee

Copyright © 2022 The Little Flower of Nashville LLC

Printed in the United States of America

Biblical references are taken from two versions: (1) The *Revised Standard Version of the Bible — Second Catholic Edition* (Ignatius Edition), copyright © 1965, 1966, 2006 National Council of the Churches of Christ in the United States of America. Used by permission. All rights reserved. (2) The *New American Bible*. © 2010, 1991, 1986, 1970 Confraternity of Christian Doctrine, Washington, D.C. and are used by permission of the copyright owner. All Rights Reserved. No part of the New American Bible may be reproduced in any form without permission in writing from the copyright owner.

Cover design by Grace Robinson

No part of this book may be reproduced, photocopied, or transmitted in any form, or by any means without the prior written permission of an owner of The Little Flower of Nashville LLC.

ISBN 979-8-218-09470-6

Gloria Deo

Our Lady
You have never failed us; thank you. Totus Tuus.

For Rosie
*It will always all be for you. You were and are a joy to our family.
Thank you for showing us the way. Lead us on, sis.
Until Heaven, my girl.
I love you.*

Mom and Dad
*My heroes. Thank you would never suffice.
We all love you — more than anything.*

Barry, Brooks, Lindsey, Grace, Quinn, Reed, Luke, James, Patrick, Noah, Maris, the sweet babies that have gone before us, and all future members of the fam.

*My heart and my crew.
"United we stand, divided we fall, we're tighter
than pantyhose two sizes too small."
To the top.*

Be it done unto me according to thy word.

Contents

Foreword by Jimmy Mitchell xi
Introduction 1
Rosemary Thérèse 7
Family Life 13
The Beginning 19
Athlete, Student, Friend 25
Suffering and Joy 37
Lourdes 47
Arrival 53
One Would Be Enough 63
The Edge of Eternity 69
The Rosie Effect 87
Rosie, the Little Flower of Nashville 93
Postscript: The Cycle of Grace 99
Acknowledgments 117

Foreword

Abandonment to divine providence is one of those spiritual principles that's nice to contemplate but near impossible to live. How can we take seriously the call to surrender when life is falling apart? How can we entrust ourselves to God's loving providence when death is prematurely knocking at our door? Is peace even possible amidst insufferable pain and confusion?

Over the course of her heroic battle with cancer, Rosie Robinson taught us that the answer to these existential questions is a resounding *fiat*: "May it be done to me according to your word" (Luke 1:38). Echoing Our Lady at the Annunciation, Rosie whispered these words in the final days of her life as she was in and out of consciousness. She wrestled with them in every conversation we had over the last two years. I believe she lived them deep down in her soul at all the most important junctures of her life.

This is the great mystery of the Cross, where suffering becomes redemption and sorrow becomes joy. Rosie's suffering was undoubtedly redemptive, as she united it with Our Lord even as her doctors' reports became less hopeful and her pain more intense. Her sorrow became joy as she put everyone at ease with her sense of humor right up to the very end. I can only imagine how frequently Rosie reflected on Our Lord's words the night before He died, as He cried out, "Father, if you are willing, take this cup away from me; still, not my will but yours be done" (Luke 22:44). What a stark reminder that abandonment is not only possible but is the source of all peace and joy. God's grace is sufficient for our every need and will carry us through every season of life unto death. Indeed, God's grace was sufficient for Rosie in her life and abundant in her death.

In fact, many of her last words are forever seared into the collective memory of family and friends. Most inspiring to me was her brief murmur coming out of a seizure one day. "Come soon, Jesus. My body is tired," she said in a moment of great exasperation but profound faith. That same day, she joked about the great adventure that awaited her in Heaven. By the grace of God she always kept humor and hope alive in her heart, even when her body was racked with pain.

Where does this kind of heroic faith originate? We could easily point to her parents, so radiant with natural virtue. We could credit her five older siblings, all of whom live the Gospel with great joy and integrity. We could point to her larger Catholic community in Nashville full of Dominican Sisters, big families, and holy priests, all of whom played significant roles in her upbringing and formation.

But perhaps it's most appropriate to explain her faith with the famous words of her patroness, St. Thérèse of Lisieux, who once wrote, "Everything is a grace because everything is God's gift. Whatever be the character of life or its unexpected events — to the heart that loves, all is well." There's no doubt that Rosie's faith was a gift from God and a gift for us all, for she seized every opportunity (including unexpected illness) to fall more in love with God and surrender herself to His providence.

We all have a great deal to learn from Rosie about abandonment, suffering, and love. Reflecting on her life and untimely death will be a source of grace for me for the rest of my life. Her suffering impacted

Foreword

countless souls, some of whom may only realize their full debt of gratitude when they meet her for the first time in Heaven. Thanks be to God for the Little Flower of Nashville, who taught us that becoming a Saint is not easy, but it is simple. It may involve debilitating pain or countless pinpricks a day, but suffering is the fast track to holiness when endured for the love of God. This was Rosie's battle cry in her final days, and it must become ours as well. In the pages that follow, you will come to know Rosie's life and especially the sequence of events that led up to her death. May her heart that loved so well right up to the very end be a source of grace for you and a reminder that God is calling all of us to be great Saints — not in spite of our suffering but through it.

Jimmy Mitchell
Feast of St. Patrick, 2022
Palm Harbor, FL

Cause I'm here to finish this race. Finish it hard. no jogging.

—Rosie

JMJ

Introduction

I have never witnessed a victory like the victory of Rosie. Yes, victory. She won so many battles and then she won the war. Rosemary Thérèse. A fiery pistol since the day she was born, with a soul as sweet as a rose. Her name fits her all too perfectly. The youngest of six and the heart of the Robinson family. We always said that she was the best of us. And in the final two and a half years of her life, she proved that she truly was and is.

I don't really even know how to begin this story. I feel it overflowing in my heart, but it's hard to put words on paper sometimes. It's hard to put an experience that is so beyond understanding into words.

I often want to wrap life up in a beautifully ornate package and then finish it off lovingly with a fancy bow. It should all look beautiful, right? After all, "We are an Easter people and Alleluia is our song!"[1] So, should life not also look beautiful for us, the good news people? I lean toward perfection. I can't help it. I just want life to be perfect; I want to make perfect choices and be a perfect person. So, what a troubling realization it is for me, a perfectionist, to learn on a daily basis how incredibly

---

[1] Pope St. John Paul II, Angelus, November 30, 1986. Vatican website: www.vatican.va.

imperfect I am. I have read many books to try and teach myself how to be more perfect, how to be like the Saints I read about. They so often seem like they have it all together, like they never lose their tempers, yell at their kids, hold grudges, and so on. If perfect people existed before me, then there are absolutely no excuses for me not being able to obtain perfection now. What an exhausting way to live, right? But how often have many of us thought that? That the Saints were just perfect on earth and did not struggle with any of the normal human limitations. That their lives were wrapped in beautiful packages and were overflowing with only the good news. That we simply can't be like them — because our lives are full of imperfections and suffering. How could I be a Saint? Me, who just yelled at my child after stepping on a floor covered in tiny Legos (truly, is there any suffering like that of stepping on tiny Legos?).

There is not a lack of desire for sanctity and beauty here, but rather a lack of knowledge: How to achieve this sanctity? How to find the good, the beautiful, and the true in a messy world and a messy life? How to understand the disconnect between being a member of the good news people, but then witnessing so much suffering and pain? Jesus Christ is the answer, and He shows us how suffering and joy are not disconnected, but rather are intertwined; the ultimate source of good news came from a cross.

Rosie simplified this even more for me years ago, at the beginning of her battle with cancer when I stated, rather dramatically, that I just couldn't keep going during a very hard pregnancy. She stared at me and then stated bluntly, "Of course you can't; God has to do it through you."

Ah, so God has to make it beautiful. Such a simple and yet humble and profound statement. A hit to the pride for all of us that carry ourselves in such high esteem. We can't make all the sufferings of life into a beautifully wrapped package, but God can do it through us. We must think of His passion as a cycle, not just a moment that occurred in ancient history. It flows through each one of us. Picture yourself beside Our Lady

Introduction

and the beloved disciple while Our Lord was on the cross. As the soldier pierced His side and blood and water gushed forth, picture yourself kneeling with the blood and water flowing onto you, flowing through you. His passion may have ended on Calvary, but it continues to flow through you, through each of us. And just as He took the horribleness of His own cross and opened the gates of Heaven to all of humanity, so He can also use our crosses for good. But we have to remember that key phrase that Rosie taught us — "He has to do it through you."

In this culture that runs from suffering and death, it is almost a breath of fresh air to learn from the perspective of a teenage girl that faced it head on. I found this short message in her phone the day before she died: "All I have to do is follow because Jesus did it first. He carried His cross first." What simplicity; what trust. When you're right in the middle of something, immersed in the demands of the present, it can be hard to process what is going on right in front of you. I often knew that Rosie was special, that she was suffering well, but I did not realize just how special until much later. Rosie was, in a word, extraordinary.

All I have is my perspective, what I witnessed, what she taught me. I keep thinking, though, that there must be a reason that God allowed me to witness her story, her life, her journey. And I have come to the simple conclusion that her mission was to change lives, starting with those of us who were privileged to be closest to her. To save souls. To initiate the "Rosie Effect." And our mission, my mission, is to share it with you. To share what we witnessed in her, to continue to spread her light. I will share what I saw on the exterior, and through her writings, Rosie herself will provide the interior, precious glimpses into her heart and thoughts. She started a journal the week before she was diagnosed with cancer, and her last entry was three weeks before she died. She has much to teach us through her writings; the timing is not a coincidence as God clearly worked through her to leave these for us. Through them she shows us that "*I have to do my best with what I have right now. To live a holy life." (October 5, 2021)* That no matter what is happening around us, our reality is a good one, that God is faithful, that He loves us, and that we can be holy and joyful through suffering.

What an honor it was to care for her during her time on this earth. What a joy to know her. We entered a valley as a family, so unsure of what it held for us, so hopeful for a mountain at the end, so trusting in our miracle. I can tell you this much: we never would have guessed what we would find there. What our mountaintop would end up looking like. But what became apparent as our journey started was that she would lead us. We may have walked into that valley side by side, many of us I am sure thinking Rosie would need us for support, but we certainly did not stay side by side. Rosie led us. For two and a half years she led us. She continues to lead us now. And I know that she will keep working for one thing: to lead us all home.

We knew in the very beginning that what God started with our family on August 9, 2019, He would complete. That God would take this "bad thing" and make it beautiful — and on October 23, 2021, God completed His work in Rosie on this earth, and perhaps on that day her biggest mission yet began. Until the hopeful day of blessed reunion we will continue to cheer from the sidelines as Rosie lights up this world. To follow in the example she herself set for us, to "run and not grow weary, walk and not grow faint" (Isa 40:31).

Rosie taught me how to live, how to suffer, and ultimately how to die. Her life holds more redemptive beauty than I have ever seen. I have never felt like a part of something so much bigger than myself, a thing I truly do not fully understand. For "the sweetness of crosses accepted with the joy of free will is a great mystery, yet very real."[2] Her story is

---

[2] Fr. Jean C. J. D'Elbée, *I Believe in Love: A Personal Retreat Based on the Teaching of St. Thérèse of Lisieux* (Manchester, NH: Sophia Institute Press, 2001), 205.

Introduction

at the heart of everything I do — she made it real for me. I pray these pages give you a glimpse into her heart and soul and that her story will inspire you. I pray that telling Rosie's story brings glory to God, gives honor to Rosie, and accomplishes what she ultimately chose to fight for: the salvation of souls. As she wrote, "*It doesn't have to be the easiest. Obviously, I would love that, but honestly we're in it this far, so let's save the most souls. Lord, I love you. Help me in everything.*" (August 26, 2021)

Rosemary Thérèse

May 30, 2002, the day that the Robinsons went three and three. We did not know that Rosie was going to be a girl — my parents wanted to wait to find out. I still remember getting the phone call that it was a girl and my grandpa taking us to the hospital to meet her for the first time. We walked into the room, and there on my mom's chest was this tiny little head with a pink hat on. I all but declared war to get to hold her first. I'll never forget seeing her face and thinking, "This is the cutest baby I have ever seen." It was all in the nose: she had the perfect nose.

Well, that perfect little baby grew and grew into a little spitfire. She had no choice: being the youngest of six, she had to learn to hold her own, and she did. Rosie was always full of so much personality. Now, we definitely did not always make it easy on her. There were occasions of all of us lifting her up and down while chanting "savages, savages" (she did not enjoy this), taping her to the floor, treating her like our own personal dress-up doll — I could go on. I wish I could remember so much more of those years when we were all younger, but they were fleeting and are a distant memory now. It's more that I remember brief moments of Rosie, and all the rest is the general memory of her spirit: who she was, how she was, and her hair. Rosie always had the very best hair. When she was a little girl it fell in perfect red ringlets and as she grew, thick red waves. It was easily the most distinguishing feature about her and the most memorable. You could look into a crowd and pick her out immediately from that beautiful halo of hair.

Rosie spent most of her childhood trying to keep up with her big brothers, Quinn and Reed. Perhaps that is where she first got her speed. She would eagerly follow in their footsteps and play their games. Then, she would retreat. She enjoyed her alone time even as a young girl and would spend hours on her own playing with her playmobile toys and lovingly setting up homes for them. Her oldest three siblings — Brooks, and Gracie, and I — doted on her. She was our little "Rose Baby," and we would treat her as such. She could be described as a quiet child, as she was certainly shy around those she did not know. But as one of her teachers stated when my mom expressed her concern about her being quiet, "Yes, she is quiet, but everyone *likes* Rosie." It is always amusing to recall that she was quiet in childhood. It could be said that she "outgrew" this as she got older, but when more closely examined I have realized that she did not. Rosie would often revert to silence and did need time alone, but she grew less silent as she grew in what I believe was virtue. She loved people and life so much that she would break out of her silence because she desired to know people, to learn who they were and walk through life with them.

Rosie's younger years were a combination of homeschooling and Catholic schooling. She was homeschooled throughout the younger grades when my parents realized that it might be the way to preserve her youth and give her a longer childhood. Her childhood was simple, and she was content and happy. We all loved her dearly. There were times, though, when it was undoubtedly hard to be the youngest. Rosie had a sensitive soul, and when she felt one of us was unkind to her she would very easily dissolve into tears and flee to her room. My mom would scold us and say, "She's very sensitive." She reminds me of her great patron, St. Thérèse, when I recall those times. St. Thérèse stated in her autobiography, *Story of a Soul*, that she herself was "overly sensitive." Her mother, St. Zélie, described her as "a charming child, very alert, very lively, but very sensitive." It's funny that the exact same description could fit Rosie as a child. She grew into her sensitivity, though, in the best of ways. She noticed things: she would ask you what was going on if she felt like something was a little off or you seemed down. Her sensitivity allowed her to grow in and show great empathy. We saw this come out more and more after her diagnosis, when she worried so much about how it would affect those around her, and in how she tried to prevent others from feeling the pain of her suffering. She felt things deeply, to her very core I think, and that is where her silent nature would appear: she would not often talk about these things, but would revert back into silence and hold all things there in her heart.

As the youngest, her life probably felt, at times, like one long car ride to and from all sorts of things for her big brothers and sisters. She went to more sporting events than the rest of us combined — a unique experience to those that are the youngest in big families. Rosie was the one child born after what could be referred to as my parents' "conversion." While they did not convert to the Catholic faith, as they were both baptized Catholics, there was a time when going to church on Sundays and grace before meals was almost the extent of our faith in action. While I think their conversion and life story could be another book on its own, I won't focus on it here because my mom would insist I take it out if I do. The main point is that there was a turning point in our family, due to the sudden falling in love with the faith that my parents experienced. This had a great effect on the life of Rosie, as she went to

The Little Flower of Nashville

daily Mass and prayed a daily rosary since she was a little girl — truly, to her, it would have been for as long as she could remember.

I would not classify her as a devout daily Mass-goer in her younger years. It is not that she complained — she was never a complainer — but she was certainly an average little girl in that she was not thrilled to go every day. But she went and would dutifully sit between my parents. The priest that said those daily Masses in the St. Cecilia chapel, Fr. John O'Neill, would always recount how he would go up to speak with Rosie and she would promptly duck and hide behind my mom or dad, her shyness coming out around people she did not know well.

I can only assume though that it is the grace from the daily sacrament at Mass and the love Our Lady must have for Rosie through her dedication to the rosary that later sustained Rosie as she was presented with her mission and cross in this life.

Rosie began to attend a traditional school again in seventh grade when she was enrolled in Overbrook, on the same campus as St. Cecilia Academy, where she would later attend high school (both schools were managed by the Dominican Sisters). It was at this time that we began to realize that Rosie was fast. She may not have seemed fast to us before, as she was usually running to keep up with her older brothers, who, as older boys, were faster than her. But when she got on that basketball court with girls her own age, she smoked them. No one stood a chance — she would run up behind a girl who may have thought she had broken away and swat the ball out of her hands. People just never saw her coming. My mom thinks that Rosie may have got some of her speed from her years spent as an Irish dancer when she was a young girl. She danced for around seven years, although she never wanted to compete. But there was always that athletic side to her: as a young girl in dance, and then as she began competing in sports. She always loved pushing herself physically and was a very determined athlete, seeing great worth in fitness and overcoming her own physical limitations.

It would be easy to go on and on about her youth, but I think that the most important part is just to capture a little of who she was then. My mom has always said we are born with our temperament and personalities; from that moment we are just who God made us to be. Rosie's little soul from day one was quiet, sensitive, fiery, and determined. Once she entered high school, who she was came out more and more as she really thrived and grew into herself.

Family Life

So much of who we are comes from our families, whether they help to shape and nurture us or whether they present challenges to overcome. I feel that Rosie's story must include a little bit of our family life and a small peek into our home: Rosie's home, her safe place, and the life and people around which she was raised and formed — namely, my parents. How could Rosie's story not include my parents? Rosie would not even be here if not for them. In the beginning it was the three of them at her birth, and in the end my parents stood faithfully by her side right before her body was taken, the three of them again. I want to welcome you into our home, our family, our lives. The gift of a family is not given for the sake of the family alone, but so that the family may become a witness to the world of the divine love that Christ Himself has poured into that family. I open those light green front doors of my parents' home to you now so that Rosie's life may not just be a gift to our family, but to yours as well.

My father is a quiet man. He will not be the first to jump into a situation or conversation, but when he does, everyone listens. He reminds me a lot of Rosie — she was like him in many ways. He doesn't ever feel the need to give his opinion. He is a deeply humble man. While he will not be the first to offer his opinion, he would be the first to ask you a question if you were over at our family's home — the first to ask how you are, to make you feel comfortable and welcome. I noticed this and admired it in him many years ago, because while I always believed his nature was predominately inclined to silence, it is even more inclined to kindness. A quiet and good-natured man. Slow to anger and very quick to reason. He is what I would call "a rock." Calm in a storm, positive, and faithful. Rosie got all of those things from him, but, perhaps the most noteworthy thing that Rosie got from Dad was his sense of humor. My dad will always keep us laughing. In the car for eighteen hours and everyone is about to lose their minds — he is making us laugh. Uncomfortable situation, sad situation, hard situation — he is making us laugh. Rosie had that same trait. There was nothing like Rosie just making us all laugh, and there was nothing like being the one to make Rosie laugh.

My dad is an incredibly hard worker. There was once a season in life in which he worked all day, came home, did the dinner/bath/bedtime routine with my mom for all of us kids, and then woke at 3:00 a.m. and did a paper route. I have never heard him complain a day in my life, though. When we would complain in the mornings about school he would say to us, "Let a smile be your umbrella on this rainy, rainy day," or, "Do it with a smile on your face and a song in your heart." Then he would laugh at his own joke and how those lines would annoy us. I remember when he would come home from a long day at work and know he had a 3:00 a.m. wake-up call waiting for him, but he would play with us anyway. He was not angry at his lack of sleep and large workload, nor lazy — he didn't come home and just turn on the TV after a long day. I have memories of him on the floor wrestling my brothers, or sitting at the table doing homework with someone. I can see him holding Rosie and Reed after those long days.

There was so much of my dad in Rosie. Rosie would often turn to my dad when she needed someone to talk to about the realities of her struggles. She would tell him the truth in regard to how she was actually feeling or what was hard. She often wanted my dad when she did not feel well and liked when he would put his cool hands on her forehead. He provided her with the same safe feeling that he has provided all of us. The same strength. He is a man of virtue, and that virtue helped form Rosie into a young girl of virtue.

My mom is a nurturer. I used to think all moms were like her and was shocked when I learned that all moms are not. She, like my dad, is a hard worker. She worked weekends as a nurse throughout my childhood. When Rosie was one year old, she became a lactation consultant and continued to work weekends. She always worked alongside my dad, and they set their schedules so that one of them would be with us while the other was working. My mom began to stay at home, though, when Rosie was a baby. My dad started his own company around that time, and she was able to quit working at the hospital, although she still worked odd jobs on the side: she cleaned houses and worked as a school nurse. Her work ethic matched that of my father, and they set quite the example for us of working as a team and achieving goals.

She would always put so much effort into making things special for us. She loved and continues to love in the details. When we woke up on any holiday — Valentine's, St. Pat's, and so on (really all of them; she did stuff for every single one) — we would each have a small pile of little gifts that was so lovingly put together for us. She has an eye for making things beautiful, so they always looked aesthetically pleasing with little bows and string. She would always seek to do the little things to help us. She would lay out clean school uniforms and make our beds — even though we were "supposed" to do all of those things. An outsider may have declared us "spoiled" by her, but it was the exact opposite. She taught us to love in the little things. That small sacrifices for others matter. That things don't have to be grand to be important and that an ordinary life, an ordinary family, and a somewhat mundane routine can be beautiful.

The oldest Robinson, Brooks, was born in 1989, thirteen years before Rosie. He would go on to become a mechanical engineer, which is perfect for his mathematical brain. He is like my dad in that he has accomplished multiple housing projects on his own and can build pretty much anything he decides he wants to. He married Lindsey, whose calm ways and thoughtfulness are most welcome in a family full of stubborn personalities. I, Hayley, followed Brooks. I went on to marry my husband, Barry, and had three sons during Rosie's time on earth — Luke, James, and Patrick. We gave Rosie her godson, James. What a gift it was to see the joy the boys brought her. Rosie loved being an aunt so much. Grace came about a year after me — another redhead. She is our artist and fashionista. She works in marketing now and thrives there, as she is a very good communicator and problem solver. Quinn's next, and I'm pretty sure he hasn't slowed down since the day he was born. He is our CrossFit athlete, a fierce competitor, and a philosopher. He carries an intensity in his soul and seeks to do all things well. Reed is our final boy. When he was six and was asked what he wanted to be when he grew up, he proudly declared, "The pope!" While I'm not sure that is in his future, he is on the right track as a current fifth-year seminarian. He desires to be a priest. He is generous, kind, and friendly. He's the type that is an immediate friend to everyone he meets. And finally, our Rosemary, "Rosie," was born; she was the final child my mom carried. There are two precious souls that never joined our family on earth, because my mom miscarried — we hope and pray we will be reunited with them one day. Together my mother and father really did work hard to create a loving home for us.

Now, it was not constantly filled with peace and abounding joy and happiness. There was struggle, preteens turning into mouthy teens, little boys being destructive, siblings' arguments, rebellion against the family rules — I could go on. But when I look back on our family home, I recall it being a safe place, an overall happy home where my parents were trying their hardest to build a good life for their family. As we one by one grew into adults it became a home filled with even more peace and laughter, as some of the daily stresses of having smaller children faded. We danced in the kitchen a lot, often to "Hooked on a Feeling" and other oldies. We teased each other often, watched a lot of football, played outside, sang "Rocky Top" loudly, and just laughed.

We would crowd around the big rectangular wooden dining table each night. There were two long benches on either side with chairs at the head and foot. Boys on one bench, girls on the other, with my parents on the ends. We'd laugh or argue our way through dinner — you just never know what family life is going to bring. And then always, at the end of each day, we'd come together for the family rosary. Through the years, our family's devotion to Mary has grown and, I think, her protection and love for us has grown alongside it. The rosary started when I was around nine or ten. We were informed that we would be going from our one decade of the rosary each night to the full rosary for Lent. Well, Lent came and went and the rosary did not go with it. Much to the despair of me and my siblings, the rosary continued every night. That's right, it was not met with pious and obedient children. It was met with grumbling, eye rolls, sibling fights, and so on. I personally took it upon myself to fall asleep during every rosary, or if I could manage it, to time it brilliantly and fall asleep before the rosary. I only see now, as a parent to young children myself, how much perseverance it took for my parents to push through and form this challenging habit. It would have been much easier, I am sure, to just quit.

Rosemary was born into this routine — she was the only Robinson child to come after the nightly rosary had already started. She simply does not remember a time without this devotion to Mary. I truly believe that our faithfulness to our Mother through the years was what saved us in many ways. She will never fail to help those who love her.

While my parents were building this home, they had no idea what it would one day hold and ultimately what would take place there. But they put the work in, and they built a strong foundation of faith, unity, love, and laughter. This foundation laid the way for Rosie to begin her own "little way." It made the road to her calvary a little lighter. For faith saved us, and unity kept us strong. And in that home on Park Lane, peace was found in the month of October, as Rosie stood on the edge of eternity.

The Beginning

It was a long journey to reach Rosie's diagnosis. Even though it was compact and all fit into about eight weeks, it still seemed to drag as we walked further into the unknown. On June 26, 2019, Rosie was experiencing symptoms that were all similar to those of allergies or a sinus infection, and she went to see her pediatrician for the first time. She received the typical treatment of antibiotics and steroids for both of those diagnoses. Neither of those medications provided much relief for her, though. She continued to have a lot of watering in her right eye, and she and my mom returned to the pediatrician two more times to try and get her some relief for what we believed was the never-ending sinus infection. This was no big deal to us though — no one ever assumed it could be anything serious. On July 26, 2019, we went on a family vacation to the new "Robinson Family Cabin," which my parents had just purchased in the Smoky Mountains. Rosie was such a trooper on vacation — she was still not feeling her best, and a few days after we arrived at the cabin her symptoms seemed to intensify. She and my parents ended up spending a good amount of that vacation trekking to one doctor after the other. It was clear that something was not right, as it was not just some minor swelling anymore, but the right side of her face was really starting to get huge. After one hike in particular, Rosie and my parents ended up at an ER in Knoxville due to intensive swelling in her face. The ER doctor there did not believe it was serious and opted to not do a CT scan, as the current theory was that she had an abscessed tooth. My parents took her to an oral surgeon, and she underwent a small procedure for the "abscessed tooth." She could no longer even smile — her face was so large and was quite uncomfortable for her. In true Rosie fashion, though, she casually ran a race in the AAU Junior Olympics five hours away from the cabin in the midst of all of these unexpected appointments.

On August 3, after three doctor's appointments, an ER trip, one small procedure in Knoxville, and increasing amounts of pain on Rosie's part, we returned home. On August 5, Rosie and my parents went from the dentist to the ER to the pediatrician and ultimately ended up in the Vanderbilt Children's Center ER, searching for answers to Rosie's swollen face. Eventually, it was determined that there was something growing in her sinus cavity, and the only way to find out what it was would be surgery to biopsy it. After a fourteen-hour day of trying to get answers, they came home, once again without answers or any relief for Rosie, but instead a scheduled surgery. What has stood out to my parents as they look back on these weeks and very, very long and challenging days is that even as she went from doctor to doctor and had people prodding her and touching her agitated face, Rosie did not complain. And so, on August 9, we all found ourselves praying that Rosie had a fungus growing in her face, but instead, it was the day that we heard the word "cancer" for the first time.

My parents were the first to receive the news — at this point, Rosie was still a minor; she had turned seventeen about ten weeks prior. Rosie was taken to recovery, and the doctors met with my parents to provide them with the initial diagnosis: the tumor was malignant, and they believed it was leukemia. I can recall, as I am sure every member of my

The Beginning

family can, with perfect clarity, where I was when my dad called me. He called each of us as they waited for Rosie to wake up. I will always remember that phone call — it was the first time I had ever heard my father cry. When Rosie woke up, my parents were taken back to her, and it was they who told her that she had cancer. They recount that she did not really have a reaction: she was silent, she was processing — she was also recovering from surgery on her face. She was released from the hospital and they brought her home, where Quinn, Reed, and I were all waiting.

We sat anxiously in the front room, watching out the window for the van to pull up. None of us knew what to say or do, but I am sure we will always remember what happened next. When the van finally pulled up, we went onto the front porch as my parents helped Rosie from the car and walked her to the house. Again, she did not say much, but as she walked through the front door and stood among the three of us, she said her first words to us: "At least no one can make me run cross country now." And we laughed. It was the first of many, many times that Rosie herself would bring lightheartedness and comfort in the midst of uncertainty and pain. She came into the house and went to the couch where we had set up a little bed for her — again, the first time of many, and a routine we would all fall into, setting up her couch bed and getting the living room all arranged to accommodate her. As she went and sat on the couch, I followed. And I will always recall our very first conversation about her future. As she sat down, I tucked her hair behind her ears (oh, how I long to do this again one day) and smiled at her. It was then, for the very first time, that her eyes filled with tears and she cried. She laid her precious head on my shoulder and cried. She said to me, "I am so scared." I responded with a meager "I know," for truly, what does one say? I played with her hair while she cried; Rosie always loved this — she loved when people played with her hair and massaged her scalp. As she stopped crying, I promised her that she would never be alone, that we would be with her every second and fight alongside her. I did not know what I was promising then, as I had no idea what her future held or how she would end up leading the way for all of us. Rosie had ceased crying and was already taking deep breaths and entering back into her determined mode. She gave herself time to be down but would never stay down long. As she would later say in an interview, "You can't control what happens to you, but you can control how you react and what you make of a situation. That is how I face it." She started this day, August 9, day one, to begin making little choices, and determination took root in her heart: she did not choose her cancer, but she would choose her own little way each day. She would choose how she reacted — and she did.

Within the next twenty-four hours, my siblings Gracie and Brooks traveled home to support Rosie after receiving this diagnosis. So we were all there. We did not do anything special. We hung around the house, mainly just sitting in the living room together, where Rosie was resting on the couch. It was simple — we were just together. On August 12, we finally received a formal diagnosis: it was not the initial leukemia that they suspected. It was, unfortunately, a much more rare cancer, one that is hardly ever seen — Rhabdomyosarcoma.

Rhabdomyosarcoma, "Rhabdo," is a rare childhood cancer, making up only one percent of all childhood cancer cases. We had, of course, never heard of it, and yet we were told it was what was currently plaguing our girl's body. On August 16, Rosie went in for her very first PET scan, CT, and met with her oncologist, who she really liked, due to his honest and blunt nature. It was on the 16th that we learned the bad news that her cancer had metastasized to parts of her bones throughout her body.

On August 20, she had her second surgery at Vanderbilt: her port was implanted, and she received two more biopsies — one of her bone

The Beginning

marrow and one of her cerebral spinal fluid. On August 21, three months after she turned seventeen and six days before the start of her senior year, she had the first MRI of her face and chemo began.

Those days passed in such a blur — one day, things were normal, and the next, it seemed Rosie was in Vanderbilt more than she was out of it. August of 2019, at least, seemed that way — it passed quickly as we received more and more information and a plan was formed. It took time, but we seemed to slowly fall into a new routine.

My dad always said that Rosie was an "outlier" from the very beginning. Nothing about her case was common — she didn't fit into any cancer category very well. I think she was an outlier in all aspects — not simply in the physical details of her illness. When asked how she felt at the start, she responded, "It's hard to put into words, but I'm not angry." How she was not angry, I do not know, but she did not often seem angry — she would occasionally have moments in which she was frustrated, as news pertaining to her future was always bad, but anger never overtook her. She never turned to bitterness or despair. While she had very real moments spanning all the human emotions, she always ended up choosing the lighthearted path, choosing humor, choosing to offer it up for her "special intention" that she never shared with us. She chose at the end of each day to come back to not focusing on the "Why am I suffering; why me?" but focusing on the "How do I want to suffer?" And Rosie freely chose to suffer well and to view her cancer through the eyes of God, not man.

> *Faith that this is what you want for me. Peace that this is my life. Not confusion for the great mystery of life. Cause it's simple it's because you love me.* — Rosie Journal, June 16, 2021

St. Thérèse writes in *Story of a Soul*, "How good God really is! How He parcels out trials only according to the strength He gives us. Never, as I've said already, would I have been able to bear even the thought of the bitter pains the future held in store for me."³ Here we were, only at the beginning, and none of us had any idea of the suffering her future held. St. Thérèse concluded this same chapter with, "I was undoubtedly big enough now to commence the struggle, to commence knowing the world and the miseries with which it was filled."⁴ We would all argue that she was not old enough; we all constantly would ask the "Why?" that she never did.

I don't know what's ahead of me in life. But I do know I want God to lead the way. You have a plan for me, I know. And it will be better than mine ever will. — July 14, 2020

It's been nine days since I found out I have cancer. This journey is going to change my life and I'm ready for it. My heart is broken that this treatment could prevent me from having kids but anything is possible with God. I'm not ready for this big change, but it's coming. I want to save souls, including my own. — August 18, 2019

---

[3] St. Thérèse of Lisieux, *Story of a Soul: The Autobiography of Saint Thérèse of Lisieux*, trans. John Clarke, OCD, 3rd ed. (Washington, DC: ICS, 1996), 47.
[4] St. Thérèse of Lisieux, *Story of a Soul*, 49.

Athlete, Student, Friend

We did not realize the athletic potential that Rosie had at first. Since she was always trailing behind her brothers, she did not usually seem abnormally fast. But once we realized it, it became so much fun. There was nothing like watching Rosie run. She would just fly. She always stood out with her very pale skin and very red hair. I have so many memories watching that red hair circle the track, slowly gaining on and passing people, or watching those long legs soar over hurdles. While she was a natural athlete and a born runner, she did not get to where she was without work. She worked so hard. She would set up a hurdle in the backyard and run and jump over and over again. She would push herself in practice and on her own. Rosie was not happy unless she knew that she gave it everything she had. This did not change after her cancer diagnosis.

I am not sure what we all expected once we learned she had cancer and saw the rigorous treatment plan that she was enduring, but I'm sure that it wasn't that she would continue to play basketball and run track — though that is exactly what she did.

The basketball season started before school even did, so Rosie began the season at the same time that she began her cancer treatments. As she wrote in her journal, *"I am NOT a quitter."* (March 17,

2020) She did worry, though, that she would have nothing to give to the team this year, but that proved to be an empty worry. Watching Rosie play basketball was one of the most inspiring things I have ever seen. As the season began, she was already a few cycles into her chemo and had a port on her left side that had been surgically placed, providing easier access for IVs and other medications. The side-effects of all the medications were in full effect, but she was still full steam ahead. She would take to the court with the same speed and determination she always showed. This time, though, she had neuropathy in her hands, and it was a struggle for her to catch the ball. As I look back, I just think, "She was so brave." She had fear and anxiety about it all, but she chose to go onto that court anyway. And as her body would tire — it happened quicker these days — she would push with all she had, never quitting until the coach pulled her out. One of my favorite things that Rosie ever said was in a voicemail to my brother Reed, in which she was recounting a story. It was after leaving a basketball practice in which her coach questioned why she was smiling, and she just laughed and answered, "Why frown when you can smile?"

In February, track season began. This would be the bigger challenge and the bigger cross for Rosie, as this was her sport: this was where her talents were and she shined on that track. Once again, just like in basketball, she was determined to try and give it all she had. She knew her future had changed. At the start of the summer, she was emailing track coaches at colleges, dreaming of her signing day at school when she would commit to one of those colleges, and practicing almost daily for the season. Here the season was, and it was not going to be the senior season she had hoped for: track in college was no longer on the horizon, and she knew her times would be slower, but she did not walk away. She walked onto that track the first day of practice and faced it all head-on — and it was hard, but she kept going:

Athlete, Student, Friend

Being slow in track is getting to me. It's worse in the moment knowing I can't go any faster. I really hope what God plans to do with my cancer is awesome, but even if it isn't I hope good comes out of it even if I never see it. —March 3, 2020

The disappointment was real and hard for her, as it was for all of us — we mourned the loss of the track career she dreamed about and that we all dreamed for her.

But she had already started offering it all to God, and she wasn't going to stop now. She kept her head up, kept laughing, and pushed on after those moments of sadness hit her:

Well today was the first track meet. I was pretty slow, but I just need to get used to the new me. I can't start complaining about it either, not an option. Parents didn't raise no sissy. God is great, beer is good, and people are crazy. That's all I've got to say. But, actually, God is great. —March 11, 2020

Even her journal entries were lighthearted.

Rosie's track coach, Bryan Picklesimer, stated:

Rosie was an ordinary high school girl, with an extraordinary drive and passion for everything she did (mixed in with a healthy dose of sarcastic wit). Everyone who knew her was gifted by her friendship, smile, and quick wit. She worked so hard in everything she did and was never satisfied with anything that she did not feel was her best. There were many moments in track where she felt she underperformed and would be close to tears with frustration. In these moments, I always knew that she was something special and that the world better pay attention, because she was about to unleash in her next event. Where someone else may have let a bad performance slide or been upset, but not done anything about it, Rosie would double down at practice the next day, ensuring that she was working hard so that she would not fail again. Her drive and desire to improve made me want to become better myself.

Rosie and Coach P had a unique relationship. He was one of the few people she would talk to about the struggles that came with cancer. She considered him a coach and a friend. Call it a blessing in disguise, but shortly after track season started, Covid hit, and even though the season had just begun, track abruptly ended. For us, this was somewhat of a relief, a silver lining. One less thing for Rosie to have to suffer through, because we all knew she would have never walked away from the season. No matter how hard it got for her, she would have been determined to finish. But now, that was one thing she did not have to do. One less cross to carry.

Before I wrote this book, I interviewed all the people we knew to be Rosie's closest friends. I wanted to hear who she was as a friend, what she was like at school, what people remembered most about her. While I knew it would be all good feedback, because I knew who Rosie was, I had no idea the role that she played in the lives of so many around her. It left me in awe as I heard time and time again the friend that Rosie was to so many. Throughout the interview process, three things remained at the top of everyone's mind and were the main things that all her friends attributed to her — joy, kindness, wisdom, and faith.

When she was fifteen, she was standing in a group of girls who were talking unkindly about another girl who was not present — you know, typical stuff for fifteen-year-old girls. Rosie, though, just calmly and bluntly stated, "Why do you all think you're so much better than her?" Now, probably only Rosie could have pulled this off and not sounded condescending and pretentious. She had a way about her that enabled her to do this. Everyone affirmed that. She was kind to everyone. She never thought herself better than anyone: she recognized that we are all wounded people, we all sin, and we all need help. In her copy of the book *Story of a Soul* we found Post-it notes, and on one she had written, "God created us all the way we are for a reason. I forget that. Whenever I am jealous of what someone else has or can do I just want to be able to tell myself not to insult God in that way." As she said in her graduation speech senior year, "Every person experiences life differently. No one can truly know what another person is experiencing. No amount of words can convey the feelings in our complicated hearts and minds. But without explaining, God embraces everything we are experiencing and guides us."

Rosie had a joy for life that came out in her love for her family, friends, and whoever she encountered. She really loved people and always wanted to bring this joy to others — she would be the first to offer a smile, a kind word, or a joke:

> *Life is beautiful, it's not going to be easy, but it's going to be beautiful. I don't know if I'm supposed to do anything with my story, but if I can help anyone I want to. Really, if all I do is help others, I'll be happy. — May 15, 2020*

She so badly just wanted to infuse the people around her with joy, to help them laugh alongside her at life. Rosie received a letter from a girl she went to St. Cecilia with toward the end of her life that I believe sums up what so many said perfectly:

> I want to thank you, Rosie. You did not know, but in 8–10 grade I struggled with severe depression, and I fought a long battle against suicide. Every time I saw you in the hallway, in class, at lunch or just anywhere, you would always go out of your way and come up to me with the biggest, most joyous smile on

your face and say "Hi, [name]!" And you would ask me about my day and how I was doing. Every time I saw you and talked with you, I felt loved, I felt wanted and I felt joy.

I heard time and time again that Rosie was simply joyful and kind to everyone she encountered. Everyone said that from freshman year, they all knew that Rosie was going to be St. Cecilia Girl, the highest honor bestowed on a senior student that St. Cecilia has to offer. It is awarded to the senior who has best portrayed the qualities of St. Cecilia all four years. And sure enough, in her senior year, it was awarded to Rosie.

After her constant kindness and joy for life, everyone spoke about how Rosie was their "go-to for advice," "the voice of reason," "the moral compass." I knew that Rosie always had a wisdom about her for her age — she was an old soul — but I would have never guessed just how much everyone relied on that wisdom. She was wise in the best way; her wisdom was rooted in mercy and unassuming in nature. She would be the last person to say she was wise and the first to crack a joke about how she wasn't if someone told her she was. I was told repeatedly that she "would put me back in line, back where I needed to be." It seems this could all be attributed to a shift in her own life, which she wrote about:

> I've changed as a person this year. I don't know if it's because of the cancer. I feel like I have life in perspective most of the time. But I'm still normal and freak out sometimes. I feel much more resigned in my emotions and more contemplative. I want to be the best I can be at everything with your help, lord. —August 2, 2020

She was wise in that she had reached a place where she recognized that while her emotions were good, she had to work to order them:

> Lord, I give you all the emotions that I'm feeling. I'm giving them to you. You make all things new. I love you. Help me to love others. Help me to do the right thing. —January 20, 2021

Athlete, Student, Friend

Now, she struggled with all the normal things that young, preteen, and teen girls do, but she always just seemed to move on quickly and to return to who she was — or she worked hard to process through things and be the person she wanted to be. She did not care very much about what people thought about her, but she cared deeply about people and wanted to help them along the path of life choose the right things. And all of her peers saw this and went to her for what they called "wisdom." One of her friends stated,

> Sometimes I wonder if everything Rosie did was intentional. While most of us become jaded and stressed down by adulthood and life, Rosie knew how to savor life and take it easy. She could play so well and create fun in the mundane. That is why I think so many of us enjoy being around children — they give us an excuse to not take life so seriously. That is to say, Rosie was far from a child. While she certainly had the ability to find joy in almost anything, her heart and mind were far beyond her age. Anytime we shared an intense conversation or had bible study, you would always be holding your breath, waiting to hear Rosie's input. I find myself missing that wisdom the most. I long for my beautiful friend that had a heart so receiving, and a mind so wise. Her words were always just right, never minced or sugar-coated. They were what you needed to hear and held you accountable.

Finally, her faith, the faith that, as I learned, inspired the faith of so many around her. Truly, not an easy feat in the time and culture when Rosie was a teenager and high school student — a time when relativism reigned and any moral objectives were frowned upon. In the main hallway at St. Cecilia there are lines of doors in a row that lead into classrooms. One of those doors, though — which looks just like the others — right in the middle of everything, does not lead to a classroom, but a chapel. I was informed that if girls wanted to go into the chapel they would try to do so quietly or when no one was looking, as it was "uncool." But not Rosie — her friends laughed as they recounted that she would swing that door open with so much gumption that it would almost hit the wall behind it, just as she would any other door. And when she came out of the chapel she would fall in line with the person nearest her and just start talking and laughing like she hadn't even been there. She made faith look natural and normal because, for her, it was. Through reading Rosie's writings, we have learned just how natural it was. Jesus was her friend, her confidant, her companion. She spoke in her letters to Him like she would anyone else — like He was sitting right next to her. She told Him all the small things, all the good and the bad: her trust in Him was that of a child's trust in their parent. Faith was not this big, complicated thing to her. It was not just a set of rules. It was a loving relationship in which she and Jesus were a team, and life was an adventure through the ups and downs.

> *Wow, the world is quite crazy. Thank you for my amazing family. I love them bunches. I'm sorry that I get in these weird funks. I let the little things bother me way too much. I need to focus on the good, the beautiful and the true. I want to grow this upcoming semester into the best version of myself at the time. To glorify you. You have given me everything. I can do anything through Christ who strengthens me. I love you, Lord. — January 8, 2021*

This relationship was something evident to the friends that surrounded her regularly. They spoke to her about faith and said that her responses would call you to where you should be and make you laugh at the same time. One of her closest friends recounted how she was telling Rosie she couldn't do a holy hour; it was just too long, too hard (we all know this feeling if we've done a holy hour), and Rosie's

Athlete, Student, Friend

response was, "Well if you can't do an hour eternity is going to be really awkward." And everyone burst out laughing at how she said it, while realizing the truth in her words. I could not even count the number of times I heard that Rosie transformed the faith lives of those around her. One friend from high school and college stated:

> One of the main reasons my faith completely transformed in college was because of Rosie. Through her example to the faith, her witness of suffering without complaining, and true joy: I knew I wanted what she had. Of course, nobody can be Rosie, but through her example, I became more attentive in Mass, involved more deeply in Discipleship and Bible Study, and engaged in deeper friendships specifically with Rosie. There are so many things that I regret not saying or doing with Rosie but as I have reflected in my own friendship with her, I think she understood that she would not be here forever and that God's will for us is greater than our own wants and plans. She lived every day as if it were last and that is something I will strive for now everyday in my own life.

And another:

> A month ago I walked back into a church for the first time voluntarily in five years. It is because of Rosie and her radiance in Christ and her passion and love for Him, even in the midst of suffering, that I came back to believe. Watching Rosie and being around her joy and kindness gave me the most precious gift of all. She helped me come home again to Christ and feel a peace and a love I have not felt in years.

If Rosie had heard these things people were saying and attributing to her, she would have just laughed and brushed it off. She did not like attention. But through her writings I can see that this is all an answer to the great longing she had to use this cross for good.

> *Everyone keeps saying they know I will do something great or that you have great things in store for me. I honestly kind of resent that, I don't know why. I'd love to do something awesome, but mehhh. If I do anything from this struggle Lord, let it be help people grow closer to you. Cause that's why we're here. I love you, Lord. — June 14, 2021*

> *Lord guide me to say the right thing to lead others to you. Please help me rest at night. Everyone dies so I'm gonna eventually and then I'll meet you. But I'm looking at you face to face right now [she was in adoration]. Lord help me to do everything to glorify you. My actions, thoughts and interactions. Help my family members and my friends in all that comes. Help me to embrace every day and every opportunity to love you and others. — August 31, 2021*

There was no shift in who Rosie was in the lives of those around her, before and after the cancer. That was continually stated. I did not realize it, but Rosie's friends did not even know for a while that she was on chemo again after her initial forty rounds. She was so worried about how it might affect them that she simply chose not to tell them. They only learned about it later. She had a huge love for her friends and found so much joy walking through life with other people. She was a true friend to many.

Rosie's determination to do her best in everything did not stop with athletics. She was an honor roll student in her time at St. Cecilia, always pushing herself to work her hardest. Now, while she was smart, she was not some kind of unheard-of genius. But what she may have lacked she made up for in hard work. Rosie pushed herself to get the very best grades she could and would be upset if she felt she did not try her hardest and could have achieved a higher grade.

Rosie went to college at the University of Tennessee at Chattanooga with the desire to be a nurse. This was not her top-choice college, or originally even in the running, but she had to choose a college close to Vanderbilt and with a hospital nearby that would be able to accommodate her chemo.

She brought her can-do attitude with her, but just like in high school, academics could often be the source of her anxiety and stress. She had such a deep desire to do all things well that it was hard for her to struggle at school. She was never upset with those around her — she was always only upset with herself if she did not do well or felt as though she did not give something everything she could:

> *I've been thinking. Dangerous, I know. I think I know why it's so hard for me to forgive myself. I think I link forgiveness too closely to making excuses. And I strongly dislike excuses. So I need to work on forgiving myself. — January 7, 2020*

> *Got a little anxious tonight but I calmed down and my besties were there for me. Help me to trust you. WE didn't manifest you, Lord. You came to earth to show yourself to us. To redeem us. Thank you for loving us. Thank you for knowing and loving everything about me. — March 2, 2021*

She had goals for her life and was working hard toward them. All Rosie ever wanted was to be a wife, a mom, and lastly, a nurse. And she saw school as a way to work hard and achieve all of these things:

> *I cried about some stuff with school while I got ready for bed. I felt lost. I need to rejoice, because every day you give me is a gift and a*

chance to love someone. Help me to make life less about me. I like that. I'm tearing up right now because I don't wake up every day and see it as a gift and I want to change that. So what if I have a big exam. I'll study, and you'll be there, and I'll be there then it will be game time, sweaty palms and all. — February 15, 2020

Suffering and Joy

Growing up my dad would always say, "What train are we on?" And then we were "supposed" to respond, "The positive train," enthusiastically. While I did not always participate, for the most part everyone jumped on board. He would then pump his arm while saying, "All aboard," and, "Chooo choo." This statement was born on one of our many cross-country road trips, when my parents would give us each a see-through plastic bin, and tell us to pack for a certain amount of days and that everything had to fit in the bin. We'd all then load up in a big rental van and head west. We saw many beauties that our country had to offer out there on each one of our "Robinsons Go West" adventures. I am so grateful for these trips now, when we spent time together in tents without internet or TVs and climbed mountains together. It was on these trips that I remember most my parents' positivity — because there's nothing like traveling across the country with moody teens to camp in tents that is going to require a little laughing at yourself and positivity, a positivity that I later saw shine through Rosie. We would spend our nights playing cards, or spike ball, then hunker down in our assigned tent. It was here in these small, everyday moments of life, amidst inconveniences and family life struggles that we all witnessed (even if we didn't realize it then) suffering with joy:

> How can we be Christians, the subjects of a King crowned with thorns, baptized in His blood, absolved so often by His blood and yet run away from the cross? That would be to forget that the cross is a Marvelous invention of Divine Mercy which gives us the occasion to prove to Jesus that we love Him. What is a love that does not prove itself? I told you that love is a choice. What merit is there in choosing Jesus if we only follow Him on a path of roses? How could we know whether it was He or the roses on that pathway that we were following? He wants to be loved for Himself, not his gifts.... Without the cross there would be many more faithful in the world; but would these be loving souls? For all eternity He wants to be able to thank us for having chosen Him, in sacrifice, for having shared His cross with Him. When He gives us something to suffer, said little Thérèse, it is because He wants a gift from us. What gift? A smile from the cross.[5]

Most of us will not carry crosses the size of Rosie's. For the majority of us, it will be those everyday life crosses — annoying people, tiny children, spouses, work, unfulfilled desires requiring patience, daily stresses, and so on. But Rosie showed each of us the way.

I can still recall in vivid detail my mother telling me to "offer it up" when I told her I didn't want to do the dishes. She used to say that phrase often. And every single time it would drive me crazy. What does that even mean, for starters?! Also, did you miss the part where I said, "I don't want to do that"? Would offering it up help my desire to not want to do those dishes in any capacity? This phrase continued to just

---

[5] D'Elbée, *I Believe in Love*, 196-197

Suffering and Joy

bring annoyance through the years, even when I became a wife and a mother. I remember thinking, "Surely by this point I would understand what that horribly obnoxious phrase means," but no dice. Still nothing. I was frustrated with myself most days, how I still could not comprehend how to offer things up in hopes that doing so would bring me a deeper, undefinable joy in the struggles that came with my vocation.

It slapped me in the face a few months into Rosie's diagnosis. She once told me she was trying hard to offer it up for a special intention — an intention that we still do not know. She would say, though, how some days it was for everyone she knew to be baptized, other days for those to come back to the faith, and some days I could tell it was all she could do to just say, "Take it, Lord," because she didn't even have the strength to think of an intention. I'm not sure what I used to think was required of me to offer something up, but Rosie showed me. It might not be easy, but it is simple. Rosie did not complain. Rosie would literally be in the middle of vomiting and would look at you and smile to make you laugh. If she was too sick or was down, she just chose to say nothing at all, rather than say something negative.

A few months into senior year was the famous St. Cecilia Spirit Week. As soon as it ended one year, you were already looking forward to it the next. Rosie's senior year spirit week began when she was about seven rounds into chemo. Her beautiful red hair, which was such a part of who she was, had started falling out and was shaved off the week before. As it fell to the ground, a few tears trailed down Rosie's cheeks, but she did not utter one word. The next week she embraced her new bald head with gusto. As spirit week was underway, the senior class chose for their theme to be the Star-Spangled Seniors. And when it was time to dress up for their theme, Rosie chose to be the bald eagle. Not only was she not complaining about the loss of her beautiful hair, but she was also laughing about it. It was not an empty laughter either: Rosie's face was lit up and she was truly joyful as she paraded around in her eagle costume, bald head shining. Suffering and joy, united in this sweet seventeen-year-old girl.

Later in the week was the powderpuff football game, a historic event and the highlight of the week. Rosie naturally refused to sit the game out and on game day not only put on her uniform and took to the field, but she let her friends paint her bald head with flames and a phrase on the back stating, "If you're reading this you're slow." Well, it turned out a lot of people were slow, and even on chemo, Rosie scored the winning and only touchdown flying down that field. Rosie lived life in the midst of suffering with a great joy: she never stopped living.

There were some days where this joy was a challenging choice, and the suffering was much harder:

> *I'm going to be completely honest. I am freaking tired. I have 4 more VAC's. I've wanted to give up today, because I'm just tired of trying. I know Jesus is sharing my burden with me always but it's easy to think I am alone. I'm crying while I write this because I know it's not true. I know You are there, but sometimes it's just hard.* — March 15, 2020

> *I got anointing of the sick today. It is for sure a comfort and reminder. "Lord save me and raise me up." He gives me courage and strength. Lord if I ever forget you are the source of everything good in my life, well let's just hope that it never happens. I'm not looking forward to VAC tomorrow, but I am ready for it to be done. Bring it on!* — May 13, 2020

No one picked Rosie up like Rosie picked up herself from these painful falls under the cross. You can see through her writings that she would fall and then re-center on God and stand again under its weight:

> *My last VAC is tomorrow. I'm ready for it to be over with. I'm ready for it though like come at me but at the same time I'm dreading*

Suffering and Joy

it. I think that thought of getting more tumors will always be there but I just have to lay it at the feet of Jesus. Lord help me tomorrow. Mary help me tomorrow. I honestly can't tell if I'm scared. I know what's coming. Help my suffering bring about a greater good, Lord. I love you. Help me to be who I am supposed to be. — June 3, 2019

Rosie worked hard to be positive throughout her battle with cancer. But she didn't stop there: she wanted her struggle to result in good.

Lord, I want to use my experience to help them come closer to you. Inspiring to lead a good life is good, but life isn't going to be complete for anyone without you. — April 22, 2020

Jesus died and gave His life. So I should be willing to do whatever He calls of me. Lord, help me come closer to you and bring others with me. — April 15, 2021

She didn't just carry her cross, but her ability to still find joy is what accomplished the mission she spoke about. Rosie never sought attention — in fact, she usually opposed it. She always just wanted to be treated normally. She never wrote on social media about her cancer, and she never wrote her blog updates. The only reason she even allowed me to write them is because she wanted people to pray for her, and she knew it was the right thing to do to let people come a little bit into her story. Only a little bit — for the most part, she kept everyone on the outskirts, including us — more than we realized. She carried her cross silently, but what she never noticed was that people began to follow her while she did. You couldn't help but follow Rosie. In her speech awarding Rosie the title of St. Cecilia Girl, the principal at the time, Sr. Anna Laura, stated:

> This year's St. Cecilia girl was recently described as "one of the most outstanding young women that I have had the privilege

to teach and coach in my thirty years at SCA." Her peers clearly share that sentiment. In fact it is rare to see our St. Cecilia girl alone because she is always surrounded by a bevy of friends and younger girls who are drawn to her exuberance and gift for finding the humor in every situation. Our St. Cecilia girl can do it all, and do it with a carefree joyfulness that makes her stand out from her competitors [referencing her track career]. She makes everyone around her calmer and happier.

Rosie recognized from very early on in her battle that she did not choose the cross, but she could choose to carry it well or she could choose to reject it. Rosie wrote in her college essay:

Since the time of my diagnosis I have realized that I get to choose to be happy and positive. It is my choice. In the beginning I thought that my life was stopping because of the cancer and everyone was going on without me. Now I have realized that just the opposite is happening. My life is still going and not stopping in any way. There was just a little bit of a bigger hurdle to jump over.

A little bit of a bigger hurdle: that is how she referred to stage four metastasized cancer at the age of seventeen. I have an image of Rosie as she realized what was happening in her life, as she saw the cross that was given to her. She didn't try to run from it, she didn't turn to God in anger — instead she leaned down, picked it up and flung it over her shoulder. Then she told everyone that we had better treat her normally, and she kept walking. She chose joy. She chose love. And when she stumbled and wanted to quit, she got back up.

In the conclusion of her speech, given graduation day of senior year, Rosie looked at her fellow classmates and their families and said:

I have learned you never see the hard things coming. But this experience has taught us that every day and every moment

Suffering and Joy

is a gift and an opportunity. God gives us each day with a chance to love and with a purpose. So, I encourage everyone to be grateful for every moment, because life is flying by. And we have the responsibility, not just the ability, to make every decision count.

During this constant battle with suffering and joy, Rosie made one more significant choice: gratitude. And after nine months of cancer treatment, she stood before everyone and reminded us all to be grateful too. Not only did Rosie try to be happy in every situation, but she tried to see the good in it. She often said she was grateful for chemo because she got to meet all the nurses who became her friends, or she was grateful for radiation because she made friends with the only other patients — a bunch of old bald men. No one told old bald guy jokes quite like Rosie. She felt since she was bald, she was one of the team. She always looked for the silver lining:

> *I've been given so much. God has given me so much. An amazing family, St. Cecilia, the opportunity to suffer. That sounds crazy, but it's changed me. Obviously, I don't enjoy feeling crappy and I told God sometimes I didn't want this, but one of the hard parts is over. That's a comfort. But I'm aware more struggles are coming my way. It doesn't make me happy, but God knows I can handle it so I'm gonna go through life believing I can (With Him I can handle it, duh stupid).* — June 16, 2020

On that same entry she had written at the top of the page, "*God is light and in Him there is no darkness.*"

She not only chose to cling to the light, but she chose to look for it. On June 28, during the summer of her remission, when she carried so much stress about college and her maintenance treatment, Rosie wrote in big letters, "*Forever I will sing the goodness of the Lord.*"

I have so much to be thankful for. Everything in my life and I mean everything. You have blessed me. Thank you so much, Lord. —November 29, 2020

Let go completely into God's love for me. To trust Him with everything. I love you so much. Thank you for all the people in my life. Help me to spread your love. Thank you for loving me unconditionally. — November 18, 2020

To suffer well, this component of trust — that Rosie so clearly displayed — is required. I love reading about trust in Rosie's writings. She always wrote about it in two ways: a simple "I trust you," or more of a prayer — "Help me to trust you." This trust that God has a plan is all that can give peace in the midst of great suffering. My trust in God has increased exponentially due to witnessing Rosie's trust in Him. She readily accepted that she could die, and she was okay with that; she did not try to escape it. She once told my mom while they were talking, "However it ends, it's going to be good." And after finding out that the cancer was in her brain she wrote, *" I trust that you can do anything, Lord. But that does not mean it's the plan for me. So I have been thinking about how I might die sooner than I thought."* (June 6, 2021) Rosie really seemed to have an understanding that God could somehow use everything about her, and all her experiences, for good. "He is capable of utilizing everything for our good and never under any circumstances would He leave us lacking in the essentials — that is to say, lacking in anything that would permit us to love more."[6] St.

---

[6] Rev. Jacques Philippe, *Searching for and Maintaining Peace: A Small Treatise on Peace of Heart*, trans. George and Jannic Driscoll (Staten Island, NY: Society of St. Paul, 2002), 44.

Suffering and Joy

Thérèse says that "the love of God turns to profit all that He finds in me." These great writings seem to point to one simple phrase, found in Scripture, where God is assuring us of this simple truth: "All things work together for good to them that love God, to them who are called according to his purpose." (Rom. 8:28)

So, with trust, what do we have to fear? This trust in God and in His love for us casts out fear — even, as Rosie shows us, fear of death. For he that trusts God has nothing to fear. Christ came to give life to humanity, and humanity in turn gave Him suffering. And yet, Jesus did not run from this suffering or call us out on our immense ingratitude; instead He accepted it and gave suffering a new power, the power of His love, rooted in redemption. That redeeming love has now given suffering power, and therefore suffering does not have to be useless. Suffering now has the power to do incredible good — or bad, depending on how we accept it. I am sure we have all seen suffering turn a person bitter, for if one spends all their time resenting suffering and trying to resist it, it can destroy him. Evil may be the root cause of suffering, but evil never has the final say. Christ gave His power of redemptive love to suffering, and now it can redeem the evil.

In contrast to the man who tries to deny his suffering, "he who accepts to put everything into the hands of God, to allow Him to give and take according to His good pleasure, this individual finds inexpressible peace and interior freedom. 'Ah, if one only knew what one gains in renouncing all things,' Saint Thérèse of the child Jesus tells us. This is the way to happiness, because if we leave God free to act in His way, He is infinitely more capable of rendering us happy."[7] Rosie may not have always been "happy" to have had cancer, but she was certainly at peace with it and it did not control her. Rosie very much chose her path, and her path was one of trust, and that trust led her to peace. She did not

---

[7] Philippe, *Searching for and Maintaining Peace*, 38.

choose her suffering, but she surrendered to it. Rosie was and is a great gift to the world; I believe she, like many courageous souls before her, spared so many of us with weaker souls. Her courage to take on this suffering is invaluable. We will never know the effects of the offerings of these brave souls until we one day enter into eternity, but we can know with confidence that the acts of love on part of these members and their willingness to sacrifice for the good of the many will save us.

Lourdes

The story of Lourdes is a beautiful one. Our Lady appeared to a young girl, named Bernadette, in the small town of Lourdes in 1858. There was nothing about Lourdes that was special — it might even be more accurate to say that there were things about it that made it particularly *not special*. It was an impoverished town set in the middle point of two much nicer towns — one would only find wealthier people there who had used it as a stopping point on their way to somewhere better. Furthermore, there was nothing about St. Bernadette that would have drawn you to her. She came from a poor family, she could not read or write, and as a young girl in the mid-1800s, most would not even bother to look at her. Her family lived in a small, one-room basement, that had been formerly used as a jail cell. She would have been considered insignificant at best.

But one day, while she was out collecting sticks in the woods, as one of her jobs, she experienced the following:

> I heard a kind of rustling sound. I turned my head toward the field by the side of the river but the trees seemed quite still and the noise was evidently not from them. Then I looked up and caught sight of the cave where I saw a lady wearing a lovely

white dress with a bright belt. On top of each of her feet was a pale yellow rose, the same color as her rosary beads.

At this I rubbed my eyes, thinking I was seeing things, and I put my hands into the fold of my dress where my rosary was. I wanted to make the sign of the cross but for the life of me I couldn't manage it and my hand just fell down. Then the lady made the sign of the cross herself and at the second attempt I managed to the same, though my hands were trembling. Then I began to say the rosary while the lady let her beads slip through her fingers, without moving her lips. When I stopped saying the Hail Mary, she immediately vanished. . . .

The third time I went the lady spoke to me and asked me to come every day for fifteen days. I said I would and then she said that she wanted me to tell the priests to build a chapel there. She also told me to drink from the stream. I went to the Gave, the only stream I could see. Then she made me realise she was not speaking of the Gave and she indicated a little trickle of water close by. When I got to it I could only find a few drops, mostly mud. I cupped my hands to catch some liquid without success and then I started to scrape the ground. I managed to find a few drops of water but only at the fourth attempt was there sufficient for any kind of drink. The lady vanished and I went back home.

I went back each day for two weeks and each time, except for one Monday and Friday, the lady appeared and told me to look for a stream and wash in it and to see that the priests build a chapel there.[8]

---

[8] St. Bernadette Soubirous, Letter to Gondrand, 1861, in *Les écrits de sainte Bernadette* (Paris: 1961), 53–59, as quoted in the Office of Readings for the feast of Our Lady of Lourdes, February 11.

Lourdes

On May 6, 2021, Rosie had her routine scans. The scans did not come back with the all-clear that we were all hoping and praying for. Rather, her MRI showed that she had a spot in her brain:

Lord, I trust you and your plan for me. I really do try hard to. There is something in my brain. So, I have to get a biopsy. I have no idea what it is. Lord, I am scared for the changes in my future that I wasn't planning on. Lord, please be with me and my family. Help us to trust you. I love you. Thank you for loving me. — May 18, 2021

I'm scared. I have no idea what to expect. But you're with me. Anointing of the sick today was beautiful. Thanks for those graces, homie. I love you! I don't feel worthy, but I know I am worthy of your love. — May 19, 2021

On May 21, she had brain surgery that confirmed the spot in her brain was a recurrence of Rhabdomyosarcoma. And so, it began again: Rosie had cancer for a second time, only this time, it was worse: brain cancer.

I have Rhabdo in my brain. Bad news. I'm scared. All I can ask Lord is for strength on this journey to persevere. Help me, Lord. I love you. — May 25, 2021

I don't like being treated like a sick person. But I've got to start offering it up now. I love you lord. Help me to use this next whatever to help you the most. — May 26, 2021

It was now even more apparent than before that Rosie needed a miracle. Her first trip to Lourdes was cancelled due to Covid, but that proved to be just a gift from Our Lady, as she had something much bigger in store for us. We began to plan in earnest that May, and Mary lined up everything perfectly for us. Every door was opened, and there

The Little Flower of Nashville

was nothing in our way: she had cleared that path and removed every obstacle — finances, Covid, passports, schedules — nothing stood in our way from getting to her. And unlike that first trip that was just going to be Rosie, Mom, and Dad, this one was planned for all eight of us, plus my youngest son, Patrick, and a very special gift from Our Lady, Fr. Ryan Adorjan. We are not by any means a well-traveled family: half of us had never even left the country at the time. No one spoke a single word of French, minus my mom's one line of "My mom lives in a white house," which would have gotten us very far, I'm sure. But then, randomly, this priest that we knew only through a mutual friend agreed over a text message to travel to Lourdes with us. He had been there before, spoke French, knew where to stay, and was going to be able to offer daily Mass for us. Now not only had Our Lady done everything to get us there, but we had a guide and easy access to the sacramental graces that we would need on this trip. And with that, eight Robinsons, a priest, and a baby set off on our great adventure.

On August 1, 2021, we crossed the ocean to Lourdes to seek Our Lady's help and intercession for Rosie. The stream that St. Bernadette once dug in the mud to find is still shooting water out of the ground today, and people come from far and wide to drink of that same water. We traveled across the globe in faith that the Mother who had been such a special part of our family all those years would help us now, in our biggest time of need. We did not know what her answer would look like, what Rosie's miracle would be, but we knew it would come, for "all things work for good for those who love God, who are called according to his purpose" (Rom. 8:28). We knew that He would take the brokenness of the cancer and create beauty. We knew that Mary would help Rosie.

And we went to leave it all at her feet. All the anxiety, unknowns, the cancer, the future — we carried it all with us and we gave it to her. And we prayed that she in turn would give us peace and faith.

Lourdes

Faith, that this is what you want for me. Peace that this is my life. Not confusion for the great mystery of life. Cause it's simple because you love us. Lord, thank you for always having my back. Help me to have conviction and strength. I love you. — June 16, 2021

Lord, this only ends two ways. I live or I die. I know that's it for everyone, but it's more on my mind. Lord, what's going to happen? I'm open to dying and that being how this is all used for good, but that honestly does make me sad. I want to watch my siblings grow old, have a family, have kids. But those are all just wants. It feels wrong to expect results from Lourdes, but also wrong not to. I know even if I am not physically healed, I will be spiritually healed. I can't believe I have a brain tumor. I love you. Thank you for loving me. — July 11, 2021

Arrival

We flew overnight on the 1st and touched down in Toulouse, France, on August 2, at 4:50 p.m. It was 9:00 a.m. to our tired bodies, but time was irrelevant at that point after traveling for so long. As we walked out of the airport the sun was shining bright, and the summer air in France was more like the fresh spring air in the States. It was not hot and humid; it was fresh and comfortable. We quickly got to our rental cars and were on our way. It was a two-hour drive to Lourdes, and it passed quickly. Our first impression of Lourdes was confusion. The streets were all single-lane and one-way with cars parked on both sides. We could see our hotel from a distance, but quite literally could not figure out how to get there. It didn't matter, though: we really did enjoy the drive, with windows down and getting our first glance of the small city. We finally made it to our hotel and up to our rooms. The hotel was marvelous, with big rooms and chandeliers and mirrors. Like much of Lourdes, it was designed with tourists in mind.

We dropped our stuff in and then went on our first outing in the city — a search for dinner. It was one of my favorite nights we had there. We just started walking. The main streets in Lourdes are paved with sidewalks on either side, but many of the side streets are cobblestone and brick. We went down the side streets and stumbled upon a pizza shop. Everyone was so friendly and quickly learned we were American. They immediately brought Lambrusco to our table and popped it open and began pouring (no one checks IDs in Europe, I learned). It was easily the greatest glass of wine I have ever had. We each got our own big pizza and just laughed, ate, and drank Lambrusco. This was the first meal we had ever shared with Fr. Ryan Adorjan, who had just traveled across the country with us. He said he could tell it was going to be a great trip at this meal, with our faces red from laughter, and maybe a little too much Lambrusco.

The next day we walked to the holy site for the first time. We would make this walk many times while we were in Lourdes; it was only about half a mile from our hotel. Down the street and past the shops that lined the roads, up one flight of stairs, and then we were there. Everything is surrounded by a large gate. There is a giant crucifix at the very front, facing you as you walk in, and then just green — green everywhere. The path splits as you walk through the gates, so that there are two paths you can take to get to the church; both are larger than your average driveway to accommodate the many pilgrims. There is a large section of green grass and flowers between the two paths and then huge fields of green on either side as you walk toward the enormous church looming in the distance. As you get closer to the church you see the back of Our Lady, not the front, for she is facing the church, not the pilgrims walking.

We made it to the statue of Our Lady and stopped to stare at her for a moment. She has her arms open wide, welcoming those who have come to meet her. It was the biggest statue of Mary that I have ever seen. We only had to walk about 50 more yards, and then we were at the front doors of the church. Upon walking in, we realized two things. First, the church was breathtakingly beautiful, and second, we were lost. The shrine of Lourdes is not large, and once you have it figured out, it is very easy to navigate, but for first-timers, it is quite confusing. As

Arrival

we learned that morning, there are two basilicas located at the shrine: the upper basilica and the lower basilica. They sit just as it sounds like they would: one on top of the other. As one can imagine, two basilicas stacked on top of each other makes for a massive building and many, many stairs — which we now had to ascend. We made it to the upper basilica and found that it was beautiful, just like the lower basilica. There were many side chapels all over the large upper basilica, and we were about 10 minutes late trying to find the right one. But, as mentioned before, there are many great benefits to traveling with a priest — one being that when he is only saying Mass for your family, he can't start without you! We successfully prepared Father on that first day for how the Robinsons tend to roll, roughly 10-15 minutes behind. We finally found Father in the St. Joan of Arc Chapel, a small detail that we would later learn was not small at all.

After Mass we explored the grounds for the first time. The holy site is made up of three churches: the original church, the much larger church built later to accommodate the mass quantities of people that were beginning to come to Lourdes, and finally, the third church, built underground, which can hold even more people. But what we were most anxious and excited to see was the grotto, the very spot where Our Lady appeared to Bernadette and the place where, in the back of a small cave, the water still springs up from the ground. The grotto was much smaller and simpler than I anticipated. There were only wooden benches for seating. The statue of Our Lady of Lourdes was placed up off the ground in a little cove, in the same spot where she appeared to Bernadette. Ivy had grown up the rocks that surrounded the statue and right under her, hewn in the rock, were the words: "Que Soy Era Immaculada Councepciou" (I am the Immaculate Conception). You could see behind the altar that was set up right under and to the left of Our Lady a little passageway that led inside the cave, which led to where Bernadette had once dug a hole. We almost didn't know what to do. After all this time, we were here, we were in the spot of miracles, and we were needing a miracle. We all just sat on those benches — we didn't talk, we didn't sit close together. I remember taking a deep breath in this moment and staring at the back of Rosie's bald head with one word on my heart: "please."

We spent the rest of the day walking around and exploring. There was a beautiful river that flowed along the side of the land, right behind the grotto: this was what Bernadette referred to as the "Gave." If you crossed the bridge over the water you were in what was referred to as the "Sanctuary." It consisted of four large outdoor spaces, with ceilings and two walls, but open on each of the ends so that you could see and walk right in. The rooms held candles, candles of all sizes, each lit. It is said that when you light a candle here you leave your special intentions at Lourdes. We picked out several candles of all sizes and lit them. We then prayed as a family for our intentions. What touched me about this simple moment was that Rosie lit several of the candles and was speaking of those she wanted to pray for. Even then, on a trip that was intended for her own healing, she was thinking about those who helped her get there and others who needed her prayers.

The next day Fr. Ryan celebrated Mass at 6:30 a.m. in the grotto. It was a once-in-a-lifetime opportunity. Once again, it was Our Lady paving the way for us, as it would not have been possible if not for some very "happy coincidences." Reed had studied at seminary and become friends with a young man who just so happened to be spending his summer working at Lourdes. He was able to book the grotto for us to have this special Mass. And through him we met the group of English-speaking seminarians who were at Lourdes. This group of young men and Reed served that Mass celebrated for us that morning in the grotto. It was a rainy and chilly morning, but the feeling of having Mass offered for Rosie in that special place could not be dampened. After Mass, Father gave Rosie the Anointing of the Sick in the grotto,

Arrival

and the morning was complete. The grace from these moments was incalculable and I am sure sustained Rosie through many hard times. Later that day we went on a tour of the museum at Lourdes, which was located near the site. We all agreed it was one of our favorite parts. Again, it was all lined up for us. The museum was closed or only open odd hours at this time, due to Covid, but thanks to our English-speaking seminarian friends who were working there, we got a special tour. There were stained-glassed windows inside, each recounting one of the Marian apparitions to Bernadette and, under each, the words Our Lady had spoken at that apparition. It was as though the whole trip was coming full circle, for we already had seen the holy space and celebrated the sacraments, and now we were getting the history and hearing the exact words Our Lady said at the grotto where we had just been. We learned that when Our Lady appeared to Bernadette, she spoke in Bernadette's local dialect and looked to be a young girl, about Bernadette's age. What a beautiful thought: Our Lady, who could have appeared as anything, chose to appear as a simple fourteen-year-old girl. She chose what would be the least frightening to Bernadette, the most simple. She will always come as we need her to. When Bernadette was asked about this moment and how Our Lady acted toward and treated her, Bernadette just simply stated, "She looked at me as one person looks at another." That surprised me in the museum that day: I am not sure what I expected, but not that. I have pondered that single line often.

I would later read in Rosie's journal that on May 9, 2020 she wrote a single paragraph: "*It's not anyone's right to pick and choose who is worthy of respect and dignity. We are all equal. We are ALL children of God.*" Our Lady treated Bernadette this way. It was simple, really, although that statement is very profound. We are each loved, and Our Lady showed that to Bernadette, without even using words: she simply looked at her "as one person looks at another."

The museum gave us a further look into Bernadette's life, and it was there that I know that, each in our own way, we began to feel connected to this little Saint, for her family was like ours in some ways. While they may have been poor, they were faithful. There is a picture in the museum at Lourdes that shows the fireplace in their one-room home, and above it hung a rosary. Her family must have surely been the place where St. Bernadette's devotion to the rosary began, a devotion that we can assume ran deep, as Bernadette carried her rosary, and that was the first thing she and Mary did together — prayed the rosary. It was the same for each of us: the devotion to Our Lady began with the family rosary, and it is something we turn to often, if only out of habit.

We went to the baths twice: that day, and on our final day there. We did as Mary had once instructed Bernadette and washed our face, our hands, and drank of the water. And then, we left. In between each of those moments at the site were many blessed family moments, full of laughter, delicious food, more wine, and lots of walking. It was the trip of a lifetime and, we would later realize, our last trip as a family before Rosie declined. We spent the last few days in France at the beach in Montpellier, and then we were back on a plane. We made a twenty-four-hour pit stop in Ireland, where we were treated like family by some dear friends, the Quinn family. It was a whirlwind of a trip, but one that was incredibly significant.

It was not until we arrived at home that I realized what had happened. The feeling of immense peace and joy, the huge hope that had grown while we traveled — part of it was gone. It was then I realized that the peace was from Lourdes itself — that while we were there it was like an invisible shield all around us. There was a peace that settled over that whole place and as soon as we were gone, I longed for it.

We arrived back home on Sunday, August 8, and the next day, on Monday, August 9, Rosie had scans. We talked about how part of us really wanted the scans for her, but the other part wanted to delay them

Arrival

and cling a little longer to the hope of her miracle. The scans came back that day showing that not only was Rosie's cancer still there, but it had progressed.

On August 19, following the scan results, on Rosie's blog, I wrote:

> I do not know why God is allowing Rosemary to suffer. But I know this: He suffered and at the end of His suffering, love triumphed — not the pain. But the love was not separated from the suffering; it was accompanied by it. Therefore, we can only assume that He allows suffering because in the end it leads to a good far greater than we can even imagine. This notion does demand a good deal of trust on our part. We must hope and believe that there is indeed a greater good than what we are able to see. That even though it might not all feel well in our souls, in the end, all will be well.

In one of his letters St. Peter tells us, "As a result, those who suffer in accord with God's will hand their souls over to a faithful creator as they do good" [1 Pet. 4:19]. It has been a great privilege to witness Rosemary handing her own soul over to our Lord. Just the other day, my four-year-old, Luke, was very upset about God not taking his own troubles away. He questioned again and again: "Why is God not taking it away?" Rosie responded to him finally — "If God wants to take it away, He will. If not, He won't." She then moved right along. While this answer was less than satisfactory for my four-year-old, it struck me. It was simple, yet incredibly profound and trusting for someone with stage four cancer.

Rosie reminds me again and again to not turn away from God in our suffering, but rather to turn towards Him. That pain and suffering can become a road that leads to God. Suffering, if anything, can remind us of our need for Him. Do not turn from it; allow the mystery of it to draw you to His mercy.

We continue to have great hope for our miracle. A miracle does not have to happen instantly to be a miracle, although that would have been cool. I began to reflect this week, though, on the fact that we already have received many miracles. Rosie beat RMS in her first ten months, while playing b-ball, completing her senior year (even made it on the honor roll) and maintaining her joy — that was a miracle. A huge miracle. It can be challenging to recall the reality that the odds were not in her favor the first time. But recognizing that also reminds us that miracles are not lacking here. They are abundant.

ABUNDANT, people. So "cast all your worries upon Him, because he cares for you" [1 Pet 5:7]. Let your prayer be one of hope. A hope that is planted deep within your hearts. Pray for Rosie's strength to be renewed; perhaps we will all find one day that her suffering saved even us. We must "walk with our feet on earth, but our hearts in Heaven" [St. John Bosco]. Trusting evermore in His great faithfulness!

None of us realized then what the miracle would be. Much more significant, though, is what Rosie wrote on August 9:

This time last year I had no idea what was going to happen to me. I still don't. But then I had to stay strong and beat the cancer. Not even stay strong, but rely completely on God. I can rely on God about everything — college, cancer, my future. — August 9, 2020

Help me to not have insecurities, because all that matters is your love and I will always have that. — August 14, 2020

The trip was amazing, I loved it. Being with the whole family in Europe. Lourdes was beautiful and so was Ireland. I'm just so grateful we got to go. We just got the MRI results back and the tumor is still there. It's grown even. So I'm very sad about that. I have

Arrival

faith in your plan God. This is not the plan I thought was for me, but obviously, it is. Lord, I'm heartbroken for my family. Help me to have the strength to get through all of this. Lord do your work through me. — August 9, 2021

Lord, do your work through me. And so it began.

Rosie at the age of 4.

Robinson Family in Ireland, from left to right: Brooks, Rosie, Quinn, Mom, Dad, Reed, Hayley and Patrick, and Gracie.

The Robinson Family children and spouses on Easter Sunday 2017.

Above: Rosie after placing in multiple events at the State Finals Track Meet.

Left: Aunt Rosie with Luke.

The Robinson Family, June of 2020 after Rosie's 40th and final round of chemo. Back row, from left to right: Barry holding James, Quinn, Mark, Jeanne Reed, Luke held by Lindsey, and Brooks. Front row: Hayley (pregnant with Patrick), Rosie, and Gracie.

The Robinson sisters in Lourdes, France.

Rosie on the cliffs of Ireland.

Mark (Dad), Rosie, and Jeanne (Mom) on the day of
Rosie's graduation from St. Cecilia Academy.

Rosie, October 17, 2021, smiling in the middle of great pain.

Mom, Dad, and Rosie in the midst of Rosie's final month, October 18, 2021.

Rosie at her visitation, dressed in white and crowned in roses, October 26, 2021.

The Cathedral of the Incarnation at Rosie's funeral Mass, October 27, 2021.

Rosemary Thérèse, Little Flower of Nashville,
a ray of joy and a fierce fighter, pray for us.

One Would Be Enough

On October 1, 2021, the feast day of St. Thérèse, we unknowingly entered the final month of Rosie's short life. Exactly one year before on that day, Rosie wrote just one line in her journal: "*Love does not calculate. — St. Thérèse.*" My mom went to visit in Chattanooga that weekend — Rosie did not feel well, which we believed to be the result of her oral chemo, but she did not let on how much she was struggling. In true Rosie fashion she was joking with my mom and did her best to keep the day light and fun. While they originally had planned to go out and enjoy Chattanooga, Rosie got sick, and they ended up spending the day in her dorm. It was a peaceful day despite Rosie feeling so poorly and is now a cherished memory for my mom.

Rosie seemed to realize the direction things were headed at this point and knew that her body was slowly shutting down. On September 14, 2021 she wrote:

> *Lord, it does not look like I am going to have a future husband, but please be with him anyway. Dr. B said I have months up to 3 years left. And they aren't going to be easy in any way. Please guide me I know you walk with me always. It's not that I don't want to see you, Lord. I'm just sad to leave my family. It's hard to look forward to somewhere none of your best friends are.*

And on September 28, 2021:

> *Lord be with everyone I love and will love. My body is still struggling. Lord thank you for everything you have given me. Help me to fulfill your purpose for me on this earth. Help me to further detach from earthly things. We both know I'll always be attached to my family though. Thank you for your merciful love. Help me to not fear the holy fires of purgatory if that's where I am going, because I want to be with you. I love you, Lord.*

And on September 29, 2021 she wrote for the final time:

> *Lord, please be with everyone I love and will love. I'm gonna freaking go to confession today. We both know I keep putting it off, sorry for that. Thank you for this day, Lord. Help me to love everyone around me. Please help my body, she's struggling a bit. Help my faith and peace in your plan strengthen.*

One week after Rosie wrote that we went on our last family trip to Wilmington, NC. Her body was still struggling, although we did not realize how much until she could no longer hide the suffering from us. On October 8, Rosie flew to Wilmington with Gracie, Mom, and Dad. She was able to walk through the airport, although it was a very slow and awkward walk: it looked as though her legs were not cooperating with her mind from an outside view. Like they were heavy and she was having to work extra hard to lift them. Losing her legs was her biggest fear, and I truly believe it was no coincidence that she lost control of those first. An incredible track athlete, an independent nineteen-year-old girl, a runner to her core, could now hardly walk.

Things went downhill quickly from there. On October 9, the very next day, she could no longer walk across the room without assistance. She was unable to keep food down, and for the first time we saw glimpses of her mind and her mouth disconnecting. She knew

One Would Be Enough

what she wanted to say, but her mouth would not say it. Quinn carried her down to the beach later that day, and we all sat getting some fresh air for a while before returning to the beach house. This trip that was supposed to be our family vacation quickly turned into somewhat of a nightmare as things rapidly devolved. We were all doing everything we could to help Rosie get comfortable, but it was challenging to be away from our own home and environment. Rosie set the bar, though, and there was no complaining. Even as she lay on an unfamiliar couch, was assisted by people on either side of her to simply walk across the room to the bathroom, and was unable to eat due to vomiting constantly, she did not utter a single complaint.

Her mind began to slow even more as the day went on. She was really struggling to speak and occasionally she would talk, but it would not pertain to anything happening around her. Or we would hear her quietly muttering and tell her we were there and try to get closer to hear what she needed. On the 10th her condition remained unchanged. Quinn carried her down to the beach again, and she sat in a chair for a moment and we all sat around her. She had laid her sweet bald head back, and her eyes were closed. You could hear the waves crashing and the breeze had made the weather a little chilly, so she was wearing her big pink sweatshirt and sweatpants, her feet buried in sand. Her clothes were hanging off her body now and it was more noticeable than ever before. It was her last time to see and hear the ocean on this earth, and I'll always cherish sitting on one side of her, holding her hand, with Gracie on the other while she experienced it. Quinn carried her back to the house where she was once again placed on the couch that had become her spot these past few days. It was this night that she would begin to mutter, and as my dad got closer to hear, that she spoke with clarity, "Be it done unto me according to thy word." I will always ponder this and carry it with me as an anthem in my own heart. She knew where this road led, and on this night, she freely accepted His will, not hers, and stepped out in faith as still more suffering awaited her. These words, originally spoken by Our Lady at the Annunciation, were now being uttered by a nineteen-year-old girl as she offered up herself to God: she did not fight it, and she did not ask why. I have never witnessed a greater act of simple faith than this one, a greater detachment from earth: she laid it all down and offered up her own self as a sacrifice, for what she had always hoped would be for the good of others.

"It is characteristic of the saint's willingness to suffer that it includes no choice: he does not choose *what* he will suffer or take one suffering to avoid another as an indirect means to pleasure. On the contrary, in his attitude in this, as in all else, is a tremendous surrender of self. He does not *choose* suffering at all, but he accepts it without conditions, because he surrenders himself to life and his personal destiny and makes no conditions. The sanctity of the saint begins in that tremendous *fiat*: 'Let it be unto me according to thy word.'"[9]

Well last week's chemo took me out. It was rough, but I never felt alone. Christ you are my rock. Mary, you are my shelter. — June 15, 2021

This faith that she had cultivated through her life would carry her through this month. On October 11, Rosie started a steroid that would blessedly help slow some of her symptoms. The same day she started it she was able to keep a little food down and speak with more ease. She would never regain the use of her legs. It was also decided on the 11th that Rosie would be unable to fly home, as was the original plan. Due to the sudden onset of her symptoms, we knew her brain tumor had grown, and it was believed the change in altitude would cause her great pain. So my parents rented a car and on October 12, they drove

---

[9] Caryll Houselander, *Guilt* (Detroit, MI: Sheed and Ward, 1952).

One Would Be Enough

the ten hours from Wilmington to Nashville to bring her home. While I can only imagine the discomfort this caused her as her back and neck were beginning to cause her pain, but she did not complain.

On the 13th, Rosie had what would be her last appointment with her oncologist. It was the second time in over two years that she had to use a wheelchair in the cancer center, but she was smiling and doing her best to talk to the nurses and those around her. Her oncologist gave her the option of trying another chemo: there was an easier version, or she could do a much more aggressive one. Neither would promise better results than the other. She would later decide to try the more aggressive one and was set to start it on Tuesday, October 19.

We were all grateful to be home at this point. Gracie and I had arrived home quicker than Rosie and my parents, as we flew, and had prepared the house as best we could for Rosie. We moved my dad's big leather recliner from the basement to the living room, took the door off Rosie's bathroom, and hung up curtains instead for easier access. Rosie was now in active pain all the time, as far as her neck and back were concerned. We would rotate ice packs on her neck and use an IcyHot roller up and down her neck and upper back to try to relieve some of the pain. She was able to walk with one person assisting on either side of her. She could not open her eyes often, as she always had double vision and it would make her sick to look around. While it was a slight improvement that she was able to walk with two people assisting and keep a little bit of food down, we would never see any large improvements, rather just a steady decline. My mom had moved a mattress onto the floor of Rosie's room and was now sleeping in there in case Rosie woke up in the night needing help with anything.

I wish I could remember every word Rosie spoke in this final month, but I cannot — but I have since realized what is more significant are the words she did not speak. Through her two-year battle with cancer, Rosie complained maybe only a handful of times, and usually only to my dad, but in this final month, where her suffering was at its peak, it seemed there was a silent resolve in her not to utter a single complaint. She did not speak one negative word. She would tell us when she was in pain, and we would try to help, but her determination to offer her suffering is something that I can now see clearly when I look back on it. It was in these first few days at home that she told me she felt bad that she was not doing anything every day — she was struggling with feeling unproductive. I attempted to gently remind her of all the souls she could be saving. It was here that her determination shone through: resolution fell over her face, she looked straight ahead, and she stated, "One would be enough."

On October 14 and 15, the rest of the family returned home. This came as a huge relief because the night of the 13th, as Gracie and I were helping Rosie from her room to the chair in the living room, her legs gave out. We caught her and sank to the ground to keep her supported. I will always cherish this minute, even though it was painful for her, as I got to hold her in my arms while she was fully conscious for the last time. Her care was now too much for just those of us that lived in Nashville, and it became more apparent each day that she would not get better. I moved back into the house this week, Brooks, Lindsey, Quinn, and Reed all moved back in from their respective places, and for the first time in years, we were all under the same roof at Park Lane once again. Her care became our focus, her days our life: she was ours and we were hers. And as a family unit we entered the final week and stood side by side on the edge of eternity.

The Edge of Eternity

As I have looked back on each of these final days, they have been filled with too many moments to mention that have forever changed me. There are simply not words when you have stood on the edge of eternity alongside your family and watched as one jumps in.

Monday, October 18, 2021

On Monday, October 18, 2021, we entered in the final week, and it became evident that we were nearing the end. Rosie could no longer move her legs and was quickly losing the ability to move her hands and arms. She was still in great pain in her neck, a pain that had kept her up the entire night before, but she was mentally sound and still could communicate. As we began this final week, that all shifted.

That morning, Rosie had her first seizure. She was in her chair in the living room, and as I was sitting on the arm I realized that she had suddenly become unresponsive, but her eyes were open. I yelled for my mom who was thankfully in the same room. She turned and began to try and talk to Rosie. We did not know what was happening, but we feared that she could have been about to die then. My mom instructed my sister-in-law, Lindsey, who was also thankfully right there, to run and get everyone. In a matter of seconds, we were all there, crowded around her chair. My father was not present, though: he was driving home from having to do some work in Knoxville. Second to witnessing Rosie go through what we would learn was a seizure, this was the worst part. We FaceTimed him, though, and placed the phone by her ear so that she could hear him. He had to pull the car over, as he was crying — we all were. But we continued to assure her of our presence, and we sang the *Ave* to her over and over. My brother Reed left the room for a short moment to call Fr. Michael Fye, who would arrive at our house shortly after the seizure ended. My brother Brooks called the doctor and was instructed it was most likely a seizure and to crush one of her medications and give it to her on a spoon. We did so and continued the whole time to speak to her and sing to her, encouraging her to come out of it. In the midst of this, I will always recall two things my mom did. First, she broke off a tiny piece of the Eucharist that had been brought over for Rosie earlier that morning that she had not yet received. She lovingly placed it carefully in her mouth and said, "Food for the journey, baby girl." Secondly, she spoke through tears to our precious girl, telling her what we all could not: that she was so loved by each of us, that she was a "joy and a delight to our whole family." I do not know precisely how long the seizure lasted, probably around four to five minutes, but I do know — it was the longest five minutes of my life. And then, Rosie came out of it. She stopped seizing and just looked around. She just looked at all of us and said, "Hey, guys." We did not tell her right then what had happened — she did not seem to know. Fr. Michael Fye arrived around this time to our home. This moment and conversation would be the last that Rosie would have, while conscious, with a priest. We all left the room and gave them time alone. It was in this conversation that Rosie stated she was "on to her next grand adventure." She had previously described Lourdes as a "grand adventure," and now it seemed she was ready for her next one. We came back shortly after and Rosie received, again, the Anointing

The Edge of Eternity

of the Sick and the Apostolic Pardon. Rosie loved being anointed. I wouldn't say she loved being sick, of course, but she grew fond of the sacrament. Her favorite moment, she told me, was when she would put out her hands and the priest would anoint them and say the words, "May the Lord save you and raise you up." She received that for the last time that morning.

After Father left, we moved Rosie out to the swing on our back porch. It was then that my mom knelt next to her and told her, "I think you might be going to see Jesus and Mary sooner than we thought, Rosie." Rosie looked over at her and asked, "Why do you think that?" My mom then told her that she had just had a seizure. She responded with "Well, that is a little scary," and she folded her sweet hands into what I can only describe as prayer hands. My mom reassured her that she was prepared, and she had nothing to be afraid of. We all sat out there on the back porch for a while. Thankfully, it was then that my dad arrived home. Rosie was glad to see him — she always wanted my dad, asking for him when he was not there. When she was restless, we would say, "Do you want Dad?" and she would nod yes, when she still could. It was a weight off of all of us, especially my mom. Eventually, we brought Rosie back into her chair and shortly after, she had her second seizure. It was just as horrible as the first, although not quite as terrifying, as we felt hopeful knowing it was another seizure and that she would come back to us.

We spent this seizure the same way we spent the first, surrounding her, talking to her, singing to her. When Rosie came out of it, we told her she had another seizure. I don't recall what my mom said next, but Rosie heard, "Do you want to say a prayer?" Rosie's mind had begun to disconnect even more, so although that's not what my mom had suggested, Rosie responded, "Sure, I will say a prayer" — she folded her hands and then said, "Lord Jesus, please come soon, my body is really tired." After being informed that she had just had another seizure, these were Rosie's words. She did not panic or cry out in despair that God had not healed her; she did not even beg for a miracle, or to be healed to stay on this earth longer. Rather, she spoke a precious prayer with such simplicity and trust. She was ready for her person to come for her, and she trusted that He would. In the final days, when it mattered most, her faith did not waiver.

It was later this day that we began our "shifts," to ensure Rosie was never alone without someone alert and awake next to her. This had not been an issue during the day, of course, and at night, my mom had been sleeping on a mattress on her floor to wake up immediately if Rosie needed her. But we realized now that Rosie needed someone always alert next to her. My dad started the night until midnight, when Brooks and Lindsey would come in and stay until 2:00 a.m.; Gracie was 2:00–3:00 a.m.; Reed 3:00–4:00; Quinn was 4:00–5:00; and at 5:00, I took over until around 7:30 or 8:00, when my dad would come in to spend the morning with her. And so, on this night, we began our constant vigil, never leaving her unattended for even a minute. It was a perpetual adoration of sorts, although it did not take place in front of the Blessed Sacrament, but at the foot of the cross. I look back on those early mornings not fondly but longingly. What I would give for just one more. One more shift to see her lying in her bed, to hold her hand, to pray with her and try to help her rest.

My mom never left. She slept on the floor and was always there if we needed to wake her up for help, which we often did, because it was also around this time that Rosie began to experience restlessness and would need medication through the night. All I can picture here is the passion of Our Lord and how Our Lady walked that with Him and then faithfully remained at the foot of the cross, as only a mother really could. Mom faithfully remained, at the foot of her child's cross. My brother Quinn journaled on this day, "It comes to us not as rhabdo in our bodies but as sorrow and raw pain in our souls. I am not sure which is worse. An illness in the body or a sword which pierces one's own soul." Mom's soul was pierced, and at the foot of the cross she remained.

Tuesday, October 19, 2021

October 19: the feast of St. John de Brébeuf, Quinn's confirmation Saint. Quinn is Rosie's confirmation sponsor. A sweet and blessed spiritual connection that keeps us united to her. Rosie's condition only intensified this day. Thankfully, she would have no more seizures for her remaining time on earth. The seizure medication was added into her daily routine. Gracie and Mom were the designated medication-givers. Gracie had created charts a few weeks prior to easily track Rosie's medicines and the times they were given to her. There were so many. At this point the goal was to attempt to minimize her pain and discomfort. My mom was Rosie's most faithful advocate in regard to medication. I will always carry with me her words during this time and how she was so insistent on talking to multiple palliative care doctors. She refused to just load her up on morphine. That could have possibly been easier for each of us, as when she was restless, it was hard, but until Rosie's final breath her mom was at her side fighting for her free will. That is not to say she did not give her all she could — she did: she did everything that was in her power to keep Rosie comfortable. But, at this point, we were told we could give her enough to essentially keep her asleep. Mom would not. We discussed it in our living room on this day. We wanted to keep her from all pain — she had already had so much. We weren't sure what was right, but Mom insisted that she needed to "be able to express herself if she wants to." And she was right.

So, we never gave her too much. We worked hard to give her just the right amount, to try and alleviate as much pain as possible but allow her also the freedom that was only God's to take. I'm grateful for that, because she truly said some amazing things in these final days.

Rosie's mental state really seemed to fade this day, and we began to see what we started calling "Rosie-isms" in full effect. We truly do not know what her interior state was most of the time, as she was losing the ability to speak. I can't say that she was "unconscious," because I don't know that she was. She would speak randomly — it was just her subconscious coming through, but she would also occasionally respond, and that makes me think that she did know what was going on around her. She had simply lost control of her body. We spoke to her often — we were always around her. We believed and hoped she could hear us. What furthered that belief was that if you told Rosie you loved her, she would say, "I love you too." At this point, it was the only thing she said that related to what was going on around her. She would also open her mouth when we said that we had medicine for her. She would open willingly and swallow.

One of our favorite stories to recount happened on this day. Mom approached Rosie and tried to brush her teeth, and Rosie simply refused. She said, "I don't trust you, Mom; you use too much toothpaste." We all laughed; it was good to hear her speaking. Mom tried again and Rosie's response this time was "Read the room, Mom." It was not that she did not want Mom to brush her teeth; she was just keeping us all laughing. The significance of this moment has become huge to me. To brush one's teeth is a simple and daily task, one that is considered beyond basic, and she could no longer do it. And her response to this was to find humor, to keep her family laughing.

She was able to move less and less. This day was the first day I could vividly recall she lost the use of her arms and the dexterity in her hands, for the most part. It seemed that after the seizures, things were declining at an incredibly rapid pace. The day before, she had spoken to us, and on this day, that was mostly gone. She still could say multiple words in a row, although they were just not related to what was going on around her. But oh how she kept us laughing. It's hard for me to even put into words what a huge thing that was. She would just burst out with hilarious one-liners about how she "freaking loved us," or "Someone holler, 'Rosie's got to go to the bathroom!' "

She yelled that last one while she was using the restroom, which had become a task that required four people. While it is a deeply personal moment, it feels like one that needs to be shared, as it was in those moments that my heart was filled with pride as I watched my family. These moments were so painful because such a simple task was no longer simple, but to watch how everyone pulled together to care for her and maintain her dignity was beautiful. At this point, one of my brothers, Brooks, Quinn, or Reed, was carrying Rosie everywhere. She could no longer control her arms, though, so they hung limply around her. As one of my brothers would so lovingly lift her, the rest of us would hold her arms and head, and the remaining members would position themselves in doorways to be sure that she was not knocked on the hard edges. Once in the bathroom, the brother that carried her would remain to help lift her, while some variation of Mom plus a sister supported her. I will always remember these moments of four of us crowded around, because there was no shame — not even from her brothers. There was simply a family working to care for our girl and seeking to do everything we could do to maintain her dignity — which was easy, because truly, I have never seen so much dignity in a human person. This routine happened many, many times each day. We later learned it was because Rosie's brain was not speaking to her bladder correctly, so she always believed she needed to use the bathroom but never could. Such a cross.

Fr. John O'Neill came over on this day to say Mass in our home for us. It was the last day that Rosie was able to receive the Eucharist in host form. Father told us in his homily that "God is very close to Rosie and loves her very, very much in a mysterious way by letting this challenge come to her. This cross could not have been carried by any but her. Consequently, Jesus is also very, very close to your family because he is allowing this cross to come onto your shoulders as well."

Wednesday, October 20, 2021

Rosie began getting very restless during the nights. She did not seem to rest with much peace anymore. I woke Mom up on most of my shifts, as did several of my siblings. Rosie would make a face that was somewhat like a grimace: she would bite her teeth together so hard. My mom told us she was trying to move. I'm sure she was correct about that, although Rosie was unable to tell us. It reminded me so much of a mother with her newborn child, to see how everything in her was geared toward Rosie in that way again. Her instincts, her body, everything. Her soul was Rosie's shield, her own needs completely forgotten as her focus was only her child. My father was my mom's support. She would lean only on him. A true and beautiful picture of the family — made for each other.

Very few people were in our home at this point. We very deliberately chose this: it was a decision to protect Rosie in the most precious days of her life, to ensure that she was being prepared for all that mattered. A dear friend who did enter our home stated it was like a halo was around Rosie, except that the halo was made up of each of us, her family. She was doing the most important work carrying her cross, approaching calvary, and we were lining the road as she walked, protecting her, encouraging her, praying for her. We were always on the sidelines watching Rosie, starting at a young age, yelling at the top of our lungs, "Run, Rosie, run!" as she raced to the finish. Here we were coming up to the most important finish line she would ever cross, back on the sidelines where we belonged.

Our home was surprisingly peaceful at this point — this will always remain striking to me. When you walk through the light green doors into my parents' house the first thing you see is a red candle, always burning during the day. It sits right under the crucifix and symbolizes what the red candle in front of tabernacles states: that Our Lord is present here. At this point, as you walked into the living room, it was different from its normal set-up. The recliner sat next to the couch, and you would find Rosie there during the day with little chairs (so we would be closer to her) all around. We set up altars all over that room and had candles and roses surrounding them. There was Mother Teresa, St. Thérèse, St. Joseph, Our Lady of the Streets, and a very large statue of Our Lady of Fatima. We would freshen the roses and change out the candles each morning so that they would burn all day. There was peace. The Saints were with us. St. Thérèse writes, "In a word, everything was sadness and bitterness, but there was still peace, always peace, reigned at the bottom of the chalice." Truly, in these moments, God reigned, as this — this is a peace the world simply could never give.

Fr. Gervan Menezes said Mass in that same room on this day — Mass was said many times in this room in front of our little altars. Rosie was no longer able to receive the Eucharist in host form. From now on, my mom would dip her pinkie finger into the chalice and rub the Precious Blood onto Rosie's lips.

Thursday, October 21, 2021

Rosie's restlessness continued as we entered this new day. We were used to our new routine at this point. Today would be the last day that Rosie would randomly speak, and for the most part, she was just asleep or unconscious — we will never know. But as always, we would continue speaking to her, reading to her, singing to her. I do not recall the exact days on which she said things, but it does seem important to share the things she said. Most often, she would mumble prayers — the Hail Mary, or she would sing part of the *Ave*. She once started singing "Oh Sacrament Most Holy" to Gracie and another time randomly joined Brooks and Lindsey as they were saying the Divine Mercy Chaplet next to her. She would come and go, sometimes aware, sometimes clearly not. But whenever she was with us, she would make us laugh or make us cry with her humble prayers.

My mom said to Rosie that she loved her, and Rosie responded, "I love you too, Mom. More than anything." The only person that ever was on the receiving end of anything negative from Rosie was my mom. As it is with most of us, mothers offer us the safest of places to bring the worst versions of ourselves. And here in this moment, it seemed that Rosie was thanking her in the best way she could for all the times my mom offered her that space.

Even in these final days she was attempting to offer us comfort when she was able to. She always worried about us, we have come to learn, and she was sad for us and the heartbreak she knew we would endure. She was always trying to protect us from the suffering of her cross. She once told Brooks in this final month, "There are good days and there are bad days. It's all going to be okay — don't worry about me."

She would say, "I love you," to each of us, and then shout things like, "I need ice cream!" And we would all laugh. Even as she was in pain and being carried, if she was awake she kept us laughing.

Fr. Mark Simpson came over for Mass on this day. We had our Mass routine down at this point. We set the altar and began, and Rosie received the Blood of Christ off of Mom's pinky finger. This day was the last day we would hear her sweet voice, although it was not lucid, as she slipped into a deep sleep this night.

Friday, October 22, 2021

Things noticeably changed on this morning. I had noticed it right away on my shift and after an hour of watching Rosie, I woke my mom up. Her breathing had changed — it was significantly slower and was clearly stomach breathing. My mom, who I'm not sure was ever really asleep due to how quickly she got up, asked for me to get my dad right away. I did so,

The Edge of Eternity

and when my dad came in he said that he had already noticed her breathing, that it had been that way for a few hours. Quinn and Gracie both confirmed it had been that way on their shifts as well. My mom asked us to gather everyone and come into Rosie's room: it was clear now that the end was approaching, although we did not know when it would come. And so, we all gathered in Rosie's room that morning, for what would be the last time. Some of us were sprawled on the floor, some of us were on the foot of her bed, and others were standing. My mom asked to hold Rosie, and she got into bed with her and we helped move Rosie into her arms. It was a preciously heartbreaking moment, as we were all aware this could very well be the last time she would ever hold her baby girl. We stayed like that for a while, Mom holding Rosie in Rosie's bed and the rest of us just sitting around. Quinn, in his usual restlessness, picked up the Bible and read John 16 aloud to us; it would not be the last time he did that. We slowly filtered out, leaving Mom, Dad, and Rosie to have some time alone. I will never forget how sad I felt leaving the three of them in that room. As a mother myself, I simply could not fathom the pain. The sword had truly pierced their hearts.

Eventually, we moved Rosie from her bed into the recliner. She did not stir at all. She was now stomach breathing only, and her mouth was slack as her body worked hard for each breath. Our vigil continued as we sat around her in the living room with all our candles lit.

Fr. Michael Fye came over midday to say Mass for us. He immediately sensed the change in Rosie, but like us he did not know how to put it into words. It was right before Mass that he said the words, "What do you do on the edge of eternity?" What does one do? How do you prepare for it? We did not know, but as my mom has always said, "When in doubt, go to Mass." And so he spoke those words and then we immediately began Mass, trusting in Jesus. It was the only thing that seemed to make sense in these final days. After Mass Fr. Fye stayed, and Fr. Daniel Steiner came over as well. Fr. Fye gave her the Apostolic

Pardon again, and the two of them prayed over Rosie and with us. Fr. Fye would reflect on this day in his homily at Rosie's funeral: "From a priestly perspective, we're in a lot of hospitals and houses in similar situations, I say this and I think all of you would agree, there was a sense of quality, or gold, a sense of victory. It was really palpable." It was palpable: it was not something that comes from mankind — it was again that peace the world could not give. It was God alone.

I like to picture our living room that day — all of us were there, sitting near or around Rosie, but also there were the angels and the Saints. The Saints that she was connected to: Mother Teresa, Thérèse, Joan of Arc, her guardian angel, other angels, Our Lady, and finally, Our Lord. She was not alone; she always believed that, that even in her loneliest times He was with her. She wrote once, "*Back in my dorm now, it's pretty lonely. But you're always with me Lord and that makes me smile. So thank you for being here.*" She wrote similar statements many times as she fought through loneliness. And there, in her most important hours, I know they were all with her, cheering her on as she was nearing the finish line, praying alongside us for her, comforting her, helping her with the grace of final perseverance.

As Friday drew to a close we did not move Rosie to her room when it was time for bed — it did not seem wise to move her very evidently struggling body. Instead, we moved all of our beds to the living room. There were mattresses on the ground everywhere, and it was like one big sleepover, although no one slept. We all sat up or just lay on one of the mattresses. We said our family rosary, and then we just waited, all painfully aware of what we were waiting for.

Saturday, October 23, 2021

Midnight came and went as we transitioned into Saturday, October 23, 2021. Nothing changed for us with the arrival of the new day as we were all still alert and in the living room. I don't think one person slept. At 3:00

The Edge of Eternity

a.m., my mom said, "Everyone come around Rosie." So we formed one tight circle around her leather recliner. She was still stomach breathing, but the gaps between each breath were becoming longer and longer. The sound of the effort needed to take a breath became louder and more mechanical, as the muscles in her diaphragm took over forcing each breath as her brain could no longer tell her body how to properly breathe. After each one we were holding our own breath, wondering if there would be another. My dad lovingly leaned over her and said, "It's okay, Rosie, you have nothing left to prove. You can let go. You're not quitting; we're so proud of you." My brother Quinn, who was up right behind her head with his arm around her, assured her of each of our presence. He told her, "We're all here, Rosie: Mom, Dad, Brooks, Lindsey, Hayley, Gracie, and Reed. We're all here." He stated those words and then at 3:32 a.m. Rosie breathed her last breath.

In the moments that followed we received what we have realized was our first miracle and rose from Heaven. Rosie died with her eyes closed, but her mouth was wide open with a slack jaw. This is a fairly common way to die when a body has lost the ability to control itself. The jaw does not close on its own after death, but a common practice is to put a rolled-up towel under someone's jaw to keep it closed before rigor mortis begins to set in. Of the seven people that surrounded her, no one saw Rosie's mouth close — it was open when she died and then suddenly, it just wasn't. It was closed, and upon her face was the sweetest and simplest smile. Her death, while so unnatural, had a unexplainable peace about it. Her body was absolutely beautiful. She was bald, unhealthily skinny, pale, and cold, and yet she was the most beautiful and peaceful person I have ever seen with that tiny smile on her face. A little smile, a little rose from Heaven.

Reed had called Fr. Gervan Menezes shortly after Rosie died, and around 4:15 a.m., he walked into our home. What a comfort Mother Church offers us in these times. He prayed with us; we all prayed for

Rosie. We prayed for her soul to that day be reunited with her person, Our Lord. We can't declare Rosie a Saint or say that she went straight to Heaven — that is for Jesus alone. We do know what He has taught us, that many will not go straight to Heaven: "The path is narrow." Most of us can probably say with confidence that we will need some time in the holy fires of Purgatory, but that girl — if anyone went straight to Heaven, it would be her. She certainly seemed to have faith in the end that she would be going to Him directly, as she asked Jesus to come. We can also have hope and trust in the sacraments and what they do for the soul. Rosie received every grace the Church has to offer before she died. She was prepared. She truly had what we should all hope and pray for — a happy and holy death.

As we all sat around her body, Father stayed with us and the hospice nurse came. We did not know what to do in this time: What does one do at a time such as this? Quinn picked up the Bible, sat on the ledge of the fireplace, and began to read John 16.

> "A little while and you will no longer see me, and again a little while later and you will see me." So some of his disciples said to one another, "What does this mean that he is saying to us, 'A little while and you will not see me, and again a little while and you will see me,' and 'Because I am going to the Father'?" [1]So they said, "What is this 'little while' [of which he speaks]? We do not know what he means." Jesus knew that they wanted to ask him, so he said to them, "Are you discussing with one another what I said, 'A little while and you will not see me, and again a little while and you will see me'? Amen, amen, I say to you, you will weep and mourn, while the world rejoices; you will grieve, but your grief will become joy. When a woman is in labor, she is in anguish because her hour has arrived; but when she has given birth to a child, she no longer remembers the pain because

of her joy that a child has been born into the world. So you also are now in anguish. But I will see you again, and your hearts will rejoice, and no one will take your joy away from you. On that day you will not question me about anything. Amen, amen, I say to you, whatever you ask the Father in my name he will give you. Until now you have not asked anything in my name; ask and you will receive, so that your joy may be complete.

"I have told you this in figures of speech. The hour is coming when I will no longer speak to you in figures but I will tell you clearly about the Father. On that day you will ask in my name, and I do not tell you that I will ask the Father for you. For the Father himself loves you, because you have loved me and have come to believe that I came from God. I came from the Father and have come into the world. Now I am leaving the world and going back to the Father." His disciples said, "Now you are talking plainly, and not in any figure of speech. Now we realize that you know everything and that you do not need to have anyone question you. Because of this we believe that you came from God." Jesus answered them, "Do you believe now? Behold, the hour is coming and has arrived when each of you will be scattered to his own home and you will leave me alone. But I am not alone, because the Father is with me. I have told you this so that you might have peace in me. In the world you will have trouble, but take courage, I have conquered the world." (John 16:16–33)

It spoke to each of us, as Scripture does. It is a gift from God to turn to in times such as these. We read it through a new lens, though, through the lens of grief and pain. How could we hear those words — that in a little while we would no longer see Him when we realized in the freshness of the pain that we would no longer see Rosie? He comforted us with His words. He reminded us that one day, our joy would once again be complete. He reminded us to take heart because He had overcome the world.

Shortly after, people from the funeral home arrived, and we each said goodbye to Rosie's body. We followed her out to the car singing the *Ave*. It was still dark outside as they loaded her body into a van. There was a peace about our home even after Rosie had died, but this part was the most unnatural and unpeaceful; when they drove away with her body. We stayed on the porch and watched until we could no longer see the tail lights.

As we walked back into the house, it felt empty. And once again, we did not know what to do, so we did what you do when you're in doubt — we went to Mass. We set up our little home altar, and as the sun rose that morning, Fr. Gervan celebrated Mass in the living room — where our youngest member had just passed into eternity, into what we hoped was the Heavenly banquet — one last time.

Fr. Gervan spent the morning with us. Thankfully, a dear friend had brought breakfast over that morning, even though she had no idea Rosie had passed. So, we ate and we talked and we prayed and we tried to rest. There was still that odd sense of peace among us, but also the emptiness that now seemed to fill the whole house without her in it.

Help me to have the strength to get through all of this. Lord do your work through me. — August 9, 2021

On August 9, 2019, God began His work in Rosie; exactly two years later, at the beginning of the end, she offered herself back to Him to continue His work, and at 3:32 a.m. on October 23, 2021, He completed it.

I'm going to be strong these remaining days of chemo. I can overcome feeling crappy and wanting to vomit. Cause I'm here to finish

The Edge of Eternity

this race. Finish it hard, no jogging. Sometimes I do just want to cry, but it's not that bad. I am going to bring some good out of all of this I don't want it to go to waste. — May 9, 2020

I don't want to be a victim. I want to be a victor, like the Saints. Life is what I make of it. And I'm not living life scared of what the future brings. —March 22, 2021

The victory was yours, Rosie.

The Rosie Effect

The following days we worked as a family to plan Rosie's visitation and burial; food poured in, and as always, our community rallied behind us. We once again, though, just kept to our home and did not have people in and out. There was a sacredness about these days, a holy silence: we just wanted to be home and together. We worked hard to plan a beautiful funeral for Rosie and to make sure it was everything she deserved. The days passed in a blur of preparation.

The day before the visitation, Mom, Gracie, and I went into Rosie's room to pick out her outfit. We picked out the white dress she wore for graduation. It was not the white dress any of us had longed to pick out with Rosie one day, but it was one she had earned: it was her wedding gown for her marriage to the ultimate Bridegroom. It represented the purity that she was able to bring with her into eternity as a gift for the Lord. She earned the honor to be buried in white. We picked out a blue shawl with light blue flowers on it to go around her shoulders, representing the Blessed Mother, to whom we had entrusted Rosie and our whole family. Rosie had once referred to Mary as "her shelter," and Mary was wrapped around her now. Nothing else could go with this beautiful outfit except for her green high-top Vans and her UT bright orange socks. This was Rosie. It all fit. She was still wearing the scapular she died in, and we selected the rosary she slept with at night for years for her to hold. She preferred the heavy beaded rosaries and would cling to them as she slept.

On October 26, 2021, we had only one thing left that we wanted to do for Rosie before her visitation that night. In pictures from her own visitation, St. Thérèse is portrayed with a crown of roses encircling her head — her sisters made this crown for her, and she is still pictured with it today. We were struck by the beauty of it. And so, Gracie and I followed suit, and on this day we made Rosie a crown of pale pink spray roses that we would later place upon her head.

The visitation was from 6:00–9:00 p.m., with a rosary at 8:45 p.m. — it was an open-casket visitation, and it would also be the first time we would get to see Rosie since her body was taken from our home. We got to the church early, all anxious to see her while simultaneously dreading it. And then, there she was, in a beautiful white casket with roses on the outside. There were over two thousand roses surrounding her body. There was still a peace and a beauty about her. We prepared ourselves and then walked alongside her into the Cathedral of the Incarnation where the visitation and funeral were held. We had set up tables in the back of the church that we had covered in some of our favorite pictures of Rosie. Rosie was placed right in front of the altar in the church, and we all lined up in age order alongside her. The night went by in a somewhat out-of-body experience. Many said that they had never seen anything like it, that people were just pouring into the church. We were told everyone waited in line anywhere from one to three hours and that it stretched out the doors and through the parking lot. It was supposed to end at 9:00 p.m.; we stayed up there until 11:30 p.m. Between the visitation and the funeral, we were told there were anywhere from two to three thousand people.

It was grace alone that kept us standing through the visitation that night. My mom later said she did not get tired and would have stood up there longer to see every person that wanted to come and see Rosie — I wholeheartedly agreed. It should have been the most exhausting night of our lives, but it was not.

The following day, October 27, 2021, we celebrated Rosie's funeral Mass and then laid her to rest.

We had planned the Mass with love, ensuring every detail had the beauty the Mass and Rosie were worthy of. There were around fifteen seminarians present, some of whom acted as altar servers for the Mass. Her funeral Mass was celebrated by Fr. Michael Fye, with nineteen other priests concelebrating. It was one of the most beautifully sacred Masses I have ever attended. Fr. Fye stated in his homily:

> This kind of peace was something I was blessed to witness with Rosie. She was facing a great mystery. A few days before I said Rosie's final Mass I was able to have a one-on-one conversation with Rosie and at the end of that conversation she was just asking very real questions. Questions we can and should all be asking. Questions about death and the great mystery. Heaven: Who do you meet there? What is it like? Of course I didn't know, but I loved it — fearlessness isn't the right word, but there was peace. There was a sense of this is real, this is going to happen, and it's good to talk about and pray about. There was a real peace.

Despite the grief and pain, Rosie's peace continued to permeate our hearts.

Just like in her care while she was living, we wanted to be the ones to surround the body that was so precious to us and to be the ones who spoke of her. So the pallbearers were my brothers, Brooks, Quinn, and Reed, my husband, Barry, our dear family friend Jimmy (whom Rosie considered a brother), and our father. And my siblings and I stepped up together at the end to give her eulogy. It was during the eulogy that we shared the term my dad coined — "the Rosie Effect."

We shared stories of Rosie's last days to illustrate how the "Rosie Effect" came to be. How a nineteen-year-old was unable to do anything because she could no longer move her body, how she eventually lost the ability to speak, and yet there she was, making us all laugh, bringing lightheartedness and cheer to the room. These moments, while seemingly ordinary, were extraordinary. These stories had the same effect on those who attended the funeral — laughter. Even at her funeral she was managing to make us all laugh, bringing a little joy — the Rosie Effect.

Come to me, all you who labor and are burdened, and I will give you rest. Take my yoke upon you and learn from me, for I am meek and humble of heart; and you will find rest for yourselves. For my yoke is easy, and my burden is light. (Matt 11:28–30)

Jesus Christ said those words, and I see them shining through in the Rosie Effect, shining through in Rosie. We were weary and burdened, but we were able to go to her, even unknowingly, and she herself made the burden lighter. She provided rest for our souls, joy for our hearts, and laughter — so much laughter. How?! It truly is mind-blowing as I look back. Her burden was not light, but she freely chose to carry it with a light heart. Rosie's body is buried right in front of the sixth station of the cross: Jesus Takes up His Cross or The Carrying of the Cross. How fitting, how well-deserved that she would be near Him in the carrying of His own cross. I sometimes have images of Rosie that play in my mind that tell the story of her journey. I can easily see her shouldering a big, heavy cross and walking on with determination in her eyes, walking toward her calvary. But then I see her reaching out and adding to her cross, making it heavier. And what she is reaching for is our pain, our suffering, and she is placing it on top of her own. Rosie could have fallen into despair and doubt. She could have constantly questioned, "Why me?" She could have been hard to be around; she could have allowed

The Rosie Effect

anger to overcome her. It would have been so easy for those things to happen, too. She could have allowed it to happen in the very beginning, when as a newly turned seventeen-year-old girl she was told she had a twenty percent chance to live five years, but she did not. Instead, she chose joy — she chose the Rosie Effect.

My brother Quinn introduced us all to the book *Man's Search for Meaning* by Victor Frankl and shared parts of it with everyone at Rosie's funeral Mass. Frankl was a neurologist, psychiatrist, and philosopher, a truly brilliant man who witnessed such brutality and suffering. In his book Frankl states, "Everything can be taken from a man but one thing: the last of the human freedoms — to choose one's attitude in any given set of circumstances, to choose one's own way."[10] Rosie understood this. She literally lived through every human freedom being slowly taken from her, but she knew she still had one choice, and she was determined to own it. She chose her own little way each day. She chose to be positive, sarcastic, loving, and witty, and ultimately she chose her faith and joy, even when she knew she was dying. Even when she was afraid. Rosie understood that at the end of the day, even when she could not brush her teeth, the biggest choice was in her own heart. And she did not squander that choice. She set the example for how we all must choose.

She chose to take this yoke upon herself, and she made a heavy burden a light weight — the Rosie Effect.

Here is the original quote from my dad. He wrote it in the letter that he drafted to be read at Rosie's funeral. No one will ever phrase it better. She really did "have it all."

"That's the Rosie Effect — just lovable — full of wit, sarcasm, playful, her smile — she had it all."

---

[10] Viktor E. Frankl, *Man's Search for Meaning*, trans. Ilse Lasch (Boston: Beacon Press, 1992), 75.

Rosie, the Little Flower of Nashville

*Lord, help me to not let
others judgments sway me.
To live life to glorify you.*
— October 30, 2020

*Help my vulnerability with you to grow
along with my love. I want to be closer to you
and to draw others closer to you.*
— October 30, 2020

Sometimes words hold great power, but often, silence holds even more. Rosie was silent often. And it is in the silence that I feel the Rosie Effect or the Spirit of Rosie. When I allow myself to really be silent and still; when the wind blows, I feel her freedom, the freedom of her choices. Even when she had lost all physical freedom, she was somehow still freer than most. When the sun rises and sets and there just are no words for the beauty, it is there that I feel her beauty. The beauty of her faith, innocence, and the trust she had in Jesus, "her person." In the open field by our home, I can feel her own openness, untainted by anger and bitter resentment. Her light; it surrounds me in this world. Her goodness, her life — they are not bound by time or gone with the death of her body — they are eternal. Our Little Flower and the Little Flower of Nashville: how she moves to fight on behalf of those she loves. That fiery little red-headed girl was always ready to fight for those she loved.

She believed in me even more than I believe in myself most days. I see her in the faces of each of my family members — like we've said, she was the best of each of us. I see her humor in my father, her ability to love in the details in my mother, her work ethic in my brother Brooks, her athleticism and determination in Quinn, her silent steadiness in Gracie, and her hope and belief in the goodness of all people in Reed. We should all strive to have small parts of Rosie in ourselves, for her virtue is truly an example we can imitate. She was not perfect, and that imperfection comforts me. She was so open in her writings about her struggles with anxiety, loneliness, and the guilt she would feel when she gave into the temptation to drink in college. But no matter where she was, she always gave it all back to Jesus in the end. She always trusted in His mercy and love for her. She would resolve to do better for Him, to not seek to escape her reality, and to work harder to not commit the same sin twice. Rosie is the perfect example of the constant struggle we all have: the effort to rise above sin and strive for interior peace, knowing that when we fall, we can turn back to Him with confidence and trust in His love for us:

> *Last night was the lowest I have ever felt in my life I think. All the bad emotions jumbled into one, hopeless, helpless, fear, sadness and despair. Just not excited for the future. But I do have a good future no matter what it is, because God has planned it and He loves me. — November 5, 2020*

Rosie, the Little Flower of Nashville

I'm super stressed about college roommate stuff. But I'm gonna focus on the present. I don't want to rush through anything. I want to savor each moment God has given me. I'm going to work with what I am given and it's going to be freaking awesome. — May 22, 2020

When faith diminishes difficulties seem deeper — I lost my faith today. I just broke down out of fear and anxiety for college. I'm sorry, Lord. I know you have me in the palm of your hand. I know you have a plan for me. Help me to not forget that. Anything is possible with God. ANYTHING. — August 4, 2020

She is a living example of how virtue and holiness is a choice, how we will always have the ability to choose: it can never be taken from us.

I can control how I respond to anything. I can't control what happens to me or how much people like me. God has a plan for me and my life. — April 10, 2020

She modeled the Christian life in that she would fall, and the next day the pages of her journal would be filled with an apology to God and conviction to do better.

All that matters in life is a relationship with Jesus. So I need to stop wasting my energy on things that don't matter. Lord, I am very self conscious of how people perceive me, but it doesn't matter what they think. Lord, there are so many moving parts in my life, help me to not continue to be carried away by them, but to regain focus on our relationship because it's very very important. I should have used more very's, but you know where I'm at. Lord I love you so much. Help me to spread your love and truly love others. — October 19, 2020

She was just a simple, little girl, with the faith of a mustard seed and the heart of a fighter.

Rosie had a chalkboard on the wall of her bathroom, right next to her shower, on which she had written, "Let the warmth of your healing love pass through my body." She never knew where this would end — no one did. But she knew no matter the ending, His love would heal her. "Love never sees anything as impossible, for it believes everything is possible and everything is permitted" (St. Thomas à Kempis). He permitted it, and along the way, she chose to not only trust Him, but to love Him and offer Him everything she had. And in the end, it was just them.

My mouth has been hurting. Big time. I think it'll be ok. Actually, I have no idea. But it's all your plan, so we got this together. Mainly you, I'm a team player though. So I'll help a bit. Well love you. Please help me sleep tonight. Help me be the best I can be. — April 6, 2021

Let go completely into God's love for me. To trust Him with everything. I love you so much. Thank you for all the people in my life. Help me to spread your love. Thank you for loving me unconditionally. — November 18, 2021

What He started in her, He completed. The race she began running on May 30, 2002, she faithfully finished on October 23, 2021. On the very first blog that was ever written on Rosie's website, I wrote: "We have great hope and peace that at the end of her mission, Rosie will be healed of all this bodily affliction and will one day receive the crown of life. 'Blessed is the man [or seventeen-year-old girl] who perseveres under trial, because having stood the test, that person will receive the crown of life that the Lord has promised' (James 1:12)."

Rosie earned her crown.

She persevered until the final breath.

A victory hard earned.

Rosie, the Little Flower of Nashville

A job well done.
A life well lived.
She "competed well... finished the race... kept the faith" (2 Tim. 4:7). And no one ever ran a race quite like Rosie.

Our sins put him on the cross, killed him. But He did it to save us. Jesus you died and rose so I could live this life. So I'm gonna live it to glorify and honor you to the best of my ability. — April 10, 2020

People always ask what we want to get out of life but I think that is the wrong question. I believe the question should be what can I give back to everyone, to the world. And that all leads to God. How can I spread God's love. By doing the ordinary with love. I need to focus on that. To make the most of all the time and opportunity I have. — March 24, 2020

She showed us how to live this life,

to really see the beauty in EVERYTHING I do and for the glory of God. That makes all the things I don't want to do more beautiful. — October 24, 2020

She made a two-year cross seem so ordinary, so normal; she taught me how to not just stare suffering in the face, but how to laugh alongside it:

Sometimes I feel like I am going through the day on autopilot. Just waiting for the next day. I don't want to live like that, but how do I change? I think by making the most of every moment. Looking for the light, happiness, or laugh in everything. God is my constant. He never changes and will NEVER change. — April 11, 2020

Thank you for teaching me that life is a joy, and every day is a gift to be lived with laughter and an opportunity to bring Glory to God.

So let's go, let's give this life everything we've got and when we fail, she showed us what to do: say sorry and start again. You only get one life, one chance: *"No excuses, no jogging."* (May 9, 2020)

BE STILL
I put my trust in you.
I am not a burden to you.
Do you have faith in me?
I can't take anyone or anything with me.
I want to run towards your beautiful embrace.
Help me to see my worth in you, not others.
I don't feel worthy.
I'm selfish. Help me to be selfless.
I want to bring others joy.
I want to be genuine.
I keep on expecting to get cancer again.
I'm sorry for choosing temporary happiness.
I know I should choose You but then I just don't.
And for that, I am sorry.
You died for me to do this.
I see my heart as being a little broken from the cancer and stronger at the same time.
I want to be the person you want me to be. Who is that? I work best with checklists. Sorry, I resort to humor. You know that obviously. I think I got my sense of humor from you. I hope I did, cause it's special. I love you lord. It's your breath in my lungs. All I have has been given to me by you. Thank you. — February 2, 2021

Run, Rosie, run! Let fall your shower of roses.

Little Flower of Nashville, pray for us.

Postscript: The Cycle of Grace

When Rosie was first diagnosed with cancer and the bad news just kept rolling in — it became more and more apparent that we would need a miracle. As the first few months passed by there were many suggestions as to Blessed candidates who need a miracle. It seemed like we could choose one and be a great team; they needed a miracle attributed to them, and we needed a miracle for Rosie.

But we never felt drawn to anyone — we never felt peace that we needed to go down that path. Instead, we felt pulled to Our Lady and St. Thérèse, Rosie's namesakes. Neither needed a miracle, but they were calling us to them. So, we went. As I look back now, it almost makes sense that it went that way. It was all a part of God's mission for Rosie. Rosie was always intended to be the miracle. Not just a part of a miracle for someone else, but the actual miracle. Throughout the months of praying to Thérèse I began to develop quite the devotion to her, as I am sure we all did. I began to speak to her as a friend, and I began to entrust Rosie to her more and more as our relationship grew. And I began to see her in our lives. She would show up here and there, sometimes in ways more obvious than others. It seemed that we did not just choose Thérèse, but she also chose us, beginning many years ago with my mom, who selected Thérèse as her confirmation Saint.

She was always working on us, moving first in the heart of my mom, then all the way down to Rosie. Helping us, loving us, preparing us for the mission that God would one day entrust to our youngest member.

When we went to Lourdes, there was a statue of St. Thérèse on the main pathway toward the church and grotto. The only other Saint on the walkway was Bernadette — which made sense, because we were in Lourdes, but there on the other side sat Thérèse. She was there, just waiting for us, to remind us that she was on our team and in the fight. The Saints are always in the fight with us, cheering us on and praying for us; we just have to open our eyes to them. While it would be strange to say that I have a favorite part of Rosie having cancer, I did learn how to see all the silver linings in her diagnosis. Rosie showed us how to do that: she was always listing off the good things that came from her cancer diagnosis:

Thank you for everyone and everything in my life. Part of me wants to resent cancer, but I see the obvious good, so I can't. — November 29, 2020

One of the good things was a renewed devotion to the Saints: a new knowledge of how closely they are working in our lives.

I have two favorite stories that seem to highlight this point. First was the day that we discovered that Mother Teresa was also working alongside us. Rosie loved Mother Teresa, so much so that she picked her as her confirmation Saint. It was not until after Rosie was diagnosed with cancer that we learned there was a connection between Mother Teresa and Thérèse.

Mother Teresa, born Agnes, had a great devotion and love for the simple ways of Thérèse. It was Thérèse that inspired her to take the name Teresa. She originally wanted to take her same name and go by Thérèse but opted for Teresa, because Thérèse was already in use by another sister. How providential though! For what would life be if she

Postscript: The Cycle of Grace

was not called Mother Teresa? The rooms of the Missionaries of Charity were kept extremely bare: they had only a bed (not a comfortable one) and a small desk, and that was it. No decorations other than those of a religious nature. But in Mother Teresa's room, we came to learn, was a picture of Thérèse, her patron and the only Saint picture she had. So, we had our girls and our Mother, closely united to each other, closely united to Rosie, cheering her on.

The second story and the final member of Rosie's Saint trio came to us the week of Rosie's death. Through reading the book on St. Thérèse written by Fulton Sheen, we came across the fact that Thérèse had a patron Saint. Some know that she had a patron, others do not — I guess it depends on how well you know the Little Flower! We did not know until this week that she was devoted to a great lady that went before her: St. Joan of Arc. In fact, she once dressed up as Joan and performed a one-woman show for her fellow sisters. In her writings she stated that as a little girl she "dreamed of being a great warrior" as Joan was. While she would grow to be a great warrior, it was certainly not the kind that little girl was dreaming of. The same day we learned of Thérèse's patroness, a pair of socks was gifted to Rosie. They were Joan of Arc socks with her quote, "I am not afraid, I was born to do this," written on them. The back of the socks had a small snippet about the Saint and revealed that her feast day was May 30, Rosie's birthday. Joan was also the first Saint that made her presence known to us in Lourdes, bright and early on our first day there when we celebrated our first Mass in France in the chapel dedicated to her. Rosie's trio was complete: a trio that I know and firmly believe was sent to Rosie to guide her on her mission, to help her along her way and would bring comfort to the rest of us.

You see, the Saints are working intricately in our lives. They are not just up there hanging in Heaven, unconcerned with us poor mortals on Earth. That was confirmed through Rosie's journey. Those strong women — how they helped her. How else could a young girl carry the weight of such a heavy cross with such grace? Her Heavenly friends never abandoned her. Just as Christ desires that we are one day all united in Him, so the Saints desire our unity with Him as well. And through our Baptism, they are one of the many gifts given to us, and they desire to help us.

"Baptism gives us participation in the prayers of the whole Church. We enter into the communion of the saints and are officially members of the Church, for the Church is the body of Christ. There is a mutual sharing of prayer, of satisfaction, and even of merit. The life of the whole Church is affected by our fervor, and we in turn live in spiritual dependence on the Church. Our incorporation in Christ means a union through him with all the other members of his Body. We are united to Our Lady, to all the saints in heaven, to all living members of the Church on earth, to the suffering members in purgatory. We can all share in their works and merits, for we are all one in Christ. In fact, no single soul on Earth works independently of the other members of the Church. The vital circulation of grace depends upon the prayers and sufferings of many souls."

So none of it was by coincidence: these were not just random occurrences; once we are baptized we are a part of this circulation of grace, we are united to the Saints — and they proved that to us. This cycle continues on in an unending flow of grace, streaming from the heart of the Father onward. I can see the grace that emitted from Rosie's suffering flowing into the cycle. While I can only hope to one day learn of all it touched, I have confidence that so much good came from it and still does.

In John 16, Jesus is telling the disciples that He will be going; He knows that they do not understand and can see that "grief has filled [their] hearts" at what He has told them (John 16:6). He then states, "But I tell you the truth, it is better for you that I go" (John 16:7). I

Postscript: The Cycle of Grace

have often pondered those words in relation to Rosie, my own life, and this cycle of grace. I have often felt her whisper in my heart, "It is better for you that I went." For I know that I can have faith and trust in the sacraments and in the Church fulfilling Her promise that Rosie can now intercede for all of us, that Rosie's suffering was not wasted.

Rosie was and is the miracle. Her prayers, her sufferings, her offerings — she so freely gave all she was. She showed us how to give and how to receive from the graces that we are all brought into by Baptism:

> *Help me to be calm. To rest in my identity as your daughter cause that will NEVER change. Uggg, that's just awesome. Lord I love you. Help me to sleep tonight. — February 21, 2021*

> *I was thinking about last year today because my cheek has been feeling weird. How am I supposed to live every day with that fear. The only thing I can think of is faith can overcome that fear. Help me have greater faith. — December 2, 2020*

> *Lord, help me not to care what others think, to not let others' judgements sway me. To live life to glorify you. Help my vulnerability with you to grow along with my love. I want to be closer to you and to draw others closer to you. — October 30, 2020*

Rosie opened almost every journal entry in two ways: "Lord, please be with my future husband right now," or "Lord, please be with everyone I love and will love." And she closed her journal entries with a simple "I love you, Lord, thank you for loving me." While she may not have sat and pondered this cycle of grace, she understood it in her heart, and she contributed always, praying for others first and opening her heart and receiving the love God was offering her.

In Rosie's final days, a Mother Teresa relic found its way to us along with a beautiful image of her, and both sat on our fireplace, along with roses and images of Thérèse. With the Joan of Arc socks on our girl's feet, the Saint squad was all present and accounted for. I have no doubts that they were present alongside her in those final days, holding on to her, cheering her on, telling her she could do this, pushing her to finish strong. And she did. As her final breath left her body, I like to picture that they were there waiting for her with open arms. Proud, just as we were, of her strength and her final perseverance.

It may have seemed small — just a young girl, in a living room in Nashville, fighting cancer until her final breath — but Heaven and earth merged that day: of that I feel sure.

Lord you are the person I talk to. I don't really open up to people. It hurts me to think of this possibility, but what if your plan is for me to die from this. What if that is how you want to impact the lives around me? I need some warning to tell my family some things. But I was created to be with you. So why should I be afraid. — July 25, 2021

I want a future here on earth, I really do. But if it's not meant to be, it's not meant to be. I love you, Lord. Thank you for loving me. — May 9, 2021

I'm gonna bring some good out of all of this. don't want it to go to waste.

— Rosie

Rosemary Thérèse Donnelly Robinson

Celebrant
Rev. Michael Fye

Concelebrants
Priests of the Diocese of Nashville

Pall Bearers

Mark Robinson   Reed Robinson
Brooks Robinson   Barry Shovlin
Quinn Robinson   Jimmy Mitchell

Readers
First Reading - Michael James Arienza
Second Reading - Jacob Hartman

THE INTRODUCTORY RITES

THE RECEPTION OF THE BODY

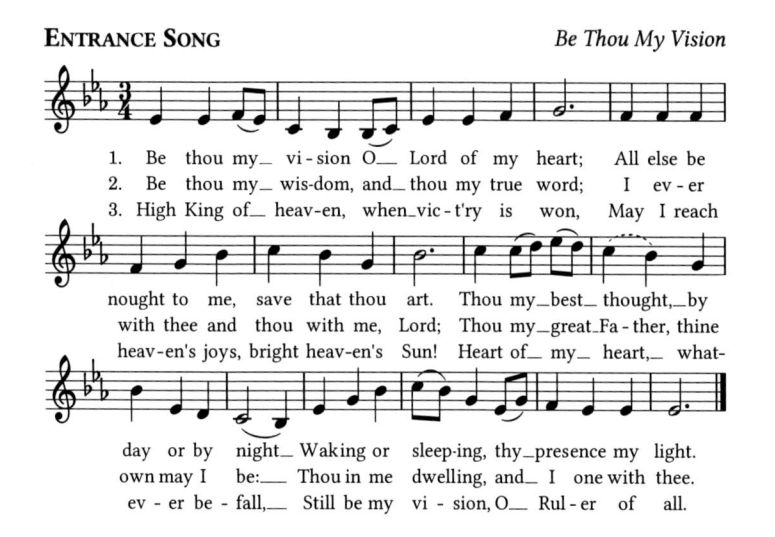

ENTRANCE SONG *Be Thou My Vision*

1. Be thou my vision O Lord of my heart; All else be nought to me, save that thou art. Thou my best thought, by day or by night, Waking or sleeping, thy presence my light.
2. Be thou my wisdom, and thou my true word; I ever with thee and thou with me, Lord; Thou my great Father, thine own may I be: Thou in me dwelling, and I one with thee.
3. High King of heav'n, when vic't'ry is won, May I reach heav'n's joys, bright heav'n's Sun! Heart of my heart, whatever befall, Still be my vision, O Ruler of all.

COLLECT

℟ Amen.

THE LITURGY OF THE WORD

READING I *Is 40: 26-31*

They that hope in the Lord shall renew their strength.

℣. The Word of the Lord. ℟ Thanks be to God.

RESPONSORIAL PSALM *Ps 62: 6-9*

℟ **My soul, be at rest in God alone,
from whom comes my hope.**

READING II   Col 3: 12-14

Charity is the bond of perfection.

℣. The Word of the Lord.   ℟. Thanks be to God.

ALLELUIA AND VERSE BEFORE THE GOSPEL   Jn 11: 25a, 26

6. F

A L-le-lu-ia,   alle-lu-ia,   alle-lu-ia

℣. *I am the resurrection and the life, says the Lord;*
whoever believes in me will never die.

GOSPEL PROCLAMATION   Jn 16: 16-33

℣. The Lord be with you.   ℟. And with your spirit.
℣. A reading from the holy Gospel according to John.
        ℟. Glory to you, O Lord.

I will see you again, and your heart shall rejoice.

℣. The Gospel of the Lord.   ℟. Praise to you, Lord Jesus Christ.

HOMILY

UNIVERSAL PRAYER (PRAYER OF THE FAITHFUL)

℟. Lord, hear our prayer.

The Liturgy of the Eucharist

Preparation of the Gifts — *Let All Mortal Flesh Keep Silence*

1. Let all mortal flesh keep silence, And with fear and trembling stand; Ponder nothing earthly-minded, For with blessing in his hand Christ, our God, to earth descendeth, Our full homage to demand.
2. King of kings, yet born of Mary, As of old on earth he stood; Lord of lords in human vesture, In the body and the blood He will give to all the faithful His own self for heav'nly food.
3. Rank on rank, the host of heaven Spreads its vanguard on the way, As the light of light descendeth From the realms of endless day, That the pow'rs of hell may vanish As the darkness clears away.
4. At his feet the six-wing'd seraph, Cherubim with sleepless eye, Veil their faces to the Presence, As with ceaseless voice they cry, "Alleluia, alleluia, Alleluia, Lord most high!"

Orate / Suscipiat

℣. *Pray brethren, that my sacrifice and yours may be acceptable to God, the almighty Father.*

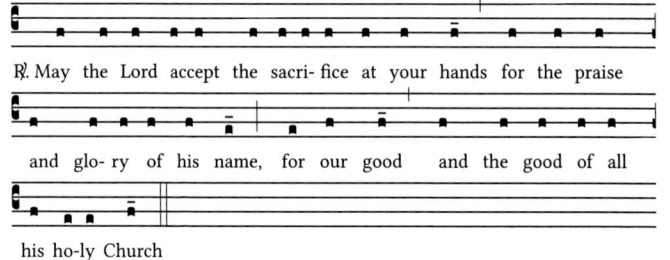

℟. May the Lord accept the sacrifice at your hands for the praise and glory of his name, for our good and the good of all his holy Church

Prayer over the Offerings

℣. ...through Christ our Lord. ℟. Amen.

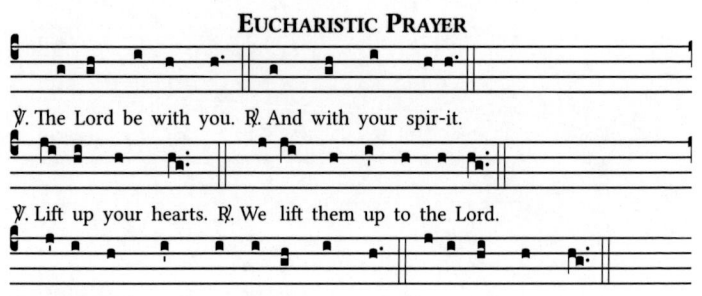

Eucharistic Prayer

℣. The Lord be with you. ℟. And with your spir-it.

℣. Lift up your hearts. ℟. We lift them up to the Lord.

℣. Let us give thanks to the Lord our God. ℟. It is right and just.

Preface

Sanctus

Anctus, * Sánctus, Sánctus Dómi- nus Dé- us Sá- ba- oth. Plé- ni sunt caé- li et térra gló- ri- a tú- a. Ho-sánna in excélsis. Bene-díctus qui vé-nit in nómi-ne Dómi-ni. Ho-sánna in excélsis.

Mysterium Fidei

Mysté-ri- um fí-de- i. ℟. Mortem tu- am annunti- ámus, Dó-mi-ne, et tu- am re-surrécti- ónem confi-témur, do-nec vé-ni- as.

Amen

The Communion Rite

Pater Noster

℣. *At the Savior's command and formed by divine teaching, we dare to say:*

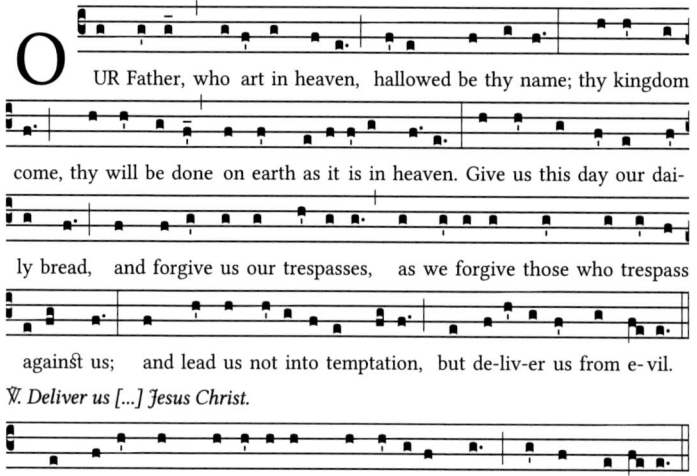

OUR Father, who art in heaven, hallowed be thy name; thy kingdom come, thy will be done on earth as it is in heaven. Give us this day our daily bread, and forgive us our trespasses, as we forgive those who trespass against us; and lead us not into temptation, but deliver us from evil.

℣. *Deliver us [...] Jesus Christ.*

℟. For the kingdom, the power and the glory are yours now and forever.

Rite of Peace

Agnus Dei

A-gnus De-i, * qui tol-lis peccá-ta mundi: mi-se-ré-re no-bis. Agnus De-i, * qui tol-lis peccá-ta mundi: mi-se-ré-re no-bis. Agnus De-i, * qui tol-lis peccá-ta mundi: dona no-bis pa-cem.

Invitation to Communion

℣. Behold the Lamb of God, behold him who takes away the sins of the world.
Blessed are those called to the supper of the Lamb.
℟. Lord, I am not worthy that you should enter under my roof,
but only say the word and my soul shall be healed.

Communion Procession

Pange Lingua

1. Pan-ge lin-gua glo- ri- ó- si Cór- po- ris mys- té- ri- um,
2. No-bis da- tus, no- bis na- tus Ex in- tá- cta Vír- gi- ne,
3. In su- pré-mæ no- cte cœ- næ Re- cúm-bens cum frá- tri- bus,
4. Ver-bum ca- ro, pá- nem ver- um Ver- bo car- nem éf- fi- cit:
5. Tan-tum er- go Sa- cra- mén-tum Ve- ne ré- mur cér- nu- i:
6. Ge-ni- tó- ri, Ge- ni- tó- que Laus et iu- bi- lá- ti- o,

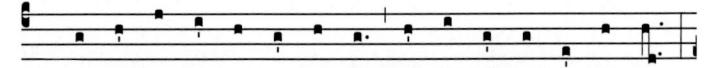

1. San- gui- nís- que pre- ti- ó- si, Quem in mun- di pré- ti- um
2. Et in mun- do con- ver- sá- tus, Spar- so ver- bi sé- mi- ne,
3. Ob- ser- vá- ta le- ge ple- ne Ci- bis in le- gá- li- bus,
4. Fit- que san- guis Christi me- rum, Et si sen- sus d é- fi- cit,
5. Et an- tí- quum do- cu- mén-tum No- vo ce- dat rí- tu- i:
6. Sa- lus, ho- nor, vir- tus quo-que Sit et be- ne- dí- cti- o:

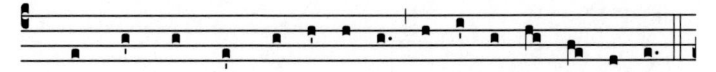

1. Fru- ctus ven- tris ge- ne- ró- si Rex ef- fú- dit gén- ti- um.
2. Su- i mo- ras in- co- lá- tus Mi- ro clau-sit ór- di- ne.
3. Ci- bum tur- bæ du- o- de- næ Se dat su- is má- ni- bus.
4. Ad fir- mán- dum cor sin- cé- rum So- la fi- des súf- fi- cit.
5. Præ- stet fi- des sup-ple-mentum Sén- su- um de- fé- ctu- i.
6. Pro- ce- dén- ti ab u- tró- que Com-par sit lau- dá- ti- o.

6. A- men.

Communion Hymn II

Panis Angelicus

1. Pa - nis an - gé - li-cus, fit— pa-nis hó - mi num, Dat pa-nis cæ - li-cus fi - gú-ris tér - mi-num. O res mi - rá - bi-lis man-dú-cat Dó-minum, Pau-per, ser-vus, et hú - mi - lis.
2. Te, tri-na Dé - i-tas ú - na que, pó - sci-mus, Sic nos tu ví - si-ta, sic - ut te có - li - mus; Per tu-as sé - mi tas duc nos quo tén-di-mus, Ad lu - cem quam in - há - bi - tas.

S Alve, Re-gí-na, * má-ter mi-se-ri-córdi-æ : Ví-ta, dulcé- do, et spes nóstra, sálve. Ad te clamámus, éxsu-les, fí-li- i Hévæ. Ad te suspi-rámus, geméntes et fléntes in hac lacrimá-rum válle. E-ia ergo, Advo-cá-ta nóstra, íl-los tú- os mi-se-ri-córdes ó-cu-los ad nos convér-te. Et Jé-sum, bene-díctum frúctum véntris tú- i, no-bis post hoc exsí- li- um osténde. O clé-mens : O pí- a : O dúlcis * Virgo Ma-rí- a.

PRAYER AFTER COMMUNION
℟ Amen.

EULOGY *All of Rosie's Siblings*

THE FINAL COMMENDATION

INVITATION TO PRAYER

SIGNS OF FAREWELL

SONG OF FAREWELL

May the choirs of an-gels come to greet you.
May they speed you to par-a-dise. May the Lord en-fold you
in his mer-cy. May you find e - ter - nal life.

Text (based on *In Paradisum*) and Music: Ernest Sands, © 1990
Published by OCP Publications, Inc., Portland OR. All rights reserved.

PRAYER OF COMMENDATION

PROCESSION

The Order of Christian Funerals
Celebration of the Eucharist

Rosemary Thérèse Donnelly Robinson

May 30, 2002 - October 23, 2021

October 27, 2021

Cathedral of the Incarnation

Nashville, Tennessee

*"I have fought the good fight,
I have finished the race, I have kept the faith."*

2 Timothy 4: 7

RECESSIONAL　　　　　　　　　　　*Precious Lord, Take My Hand*
　　　　　　　　　　　　　　　　　　　　Soloist: Maria Price Bush

Precious Lord, take my hand, Lead me on, let me stand
I'm tired, I'm weak, I'm 'lone
Through the storm, through the night, Lead me on to the light
Take my hand precious Lord, lead me home

When my way grows drear precious Lord linger near
When my light is almost gone
Hear my cry, hear my call, Hold my hand lest I fall
Take my hand precious Lord, lead me home

When the darkness appears and the night draws near
And the day is past and gone
At the river I stand, Guide my feet, hold my hand
Take my hand precious Lord, lead me home

Precious Lord, take my hand, Lead me on, let me stand
I'm tired, I'm weak, I'm 'lone
Through the storm, through the night, Lead me on to the light
Take my hand precious Lord, lead me home

Lyrics & Music by Thomas Dorsey, 1899-1993

RECESSIONAL   *O God Beyond All Praising*

1. O God beyond all praising, We worship you today
2. The flow'r of earthly splendor In time must surely die,
3. Then hear, O gracious Savior, Accept the love we bring,

And sing the love amazing That songs cannot repay;
Its fragile bloom surrender To you, the Lord most high;
That we who know your favor May serve you as our King;

For we can only wonder At ev'ry gift you send,
But hidden from all nature Th'eternal seed is sown,
And whether our tomorrows Be filled with good or ill,

At blessings without number And mercies without end:
Though small in mortal stature, To heaven's garden grown:
We'll triumph through our sorrows And rise to bless you still:

We lift our hearts before you And wait upon your word,
For Christ the man from heaven From death has set us free,
To marvel at your beauty And glory in your ways,

We honor and adore you, Our great and mighty Lord.
And we through him are given The final victory.
And make a joyful duty Our sacrifice of praise.

Our Lady of Fatima once said to three small children, "Will you offer yourselves to God and bear all the sufferings He sends you? In atonement for all the sins that offend Him? And for the conversion of sinners?" The children said, "We will." "Then you will have a great deal to suffer, but the grace of God will be with you and strengthen you." May we all have the courage to echo the children's "we will" when God asks great things of us. Our Lady showed us the way with her *fiat*, which continues to echo even now. It echoes in the faithful who trust in God's promises; it echoed in Rosie every day and in her final days as she followed in Our Lady's footsteps with her own "Be it done unto me according to thy word." May her story help inspire you to do the same, to respond in faith with your own yes to whatever God asks of you. Thank you for reading Rosie's story. Now go, do not be afraid, and set this world on fire with echoes of your own *fiat*. Rosie will show you the way.

Acknowledgments

To Shawn and Bunny, the first believers in this book and its mission, thank you. I could not have done this without your support, coffee dates, and love. Our family cherishes your friendship so much. To my cousin, Karen Metzinger, who was one of the first to read this book and provide much needed honest feedback in its early stages. Thank you for lending your talents and time to this book and for the love you showered upon Rosie in her time of sickness. To Jimmy Mitchell, thank you for being a part of this project but more importantly for being a big brother to us all through many years of friendship. To Marissa Bulso, who has been editing my work since senior year yearbook, thank you for loving Rosie and her story so well.

To Gino and Kathy Bulso, whose generosity began our planning for our family's great adventure to Lourdes and to all who helped make the trip possible.

To Fr. Ryan Adjoran, a wonderful father, friend, and peer. Thank you for all you did for our family and most importantly for Rosie.

To Fr. Michael Fye, Fr. Rhodes Bolster, Fr. Mark Simpson, Fr. Gervan Menezes, Fr. John O'Neill, Fr. Luke Wilgenbusch, Fr. Daniel Steiner, and Fr. Jayd Neely. Thank you for being fathers to us in our time of need. Thank you for bringing the sacraments to Rosie and our family every day in her final month.

To the Nashville Dominicans, thank you for being present to Rosie and to our family in every way these past years. You all have been a constant gift to us.

To Rachel Simpson, whose attention to detail saved me. Thank you for giving so generously of your time and talent.

To Nora Malone, who has the patience of a saint. Thank you for working so hard in the final weeks of this process to perfect every small detail of this book.

To every member of Team Rosie, this journey would have been much harder without each of you. We could not have walked this road with Rosie without your love and support.